Building a Sustainable and Desirable Economy-in-Society-in-Nature

Cover images:

(Left Top) by Eric Rasmussen/InSTEDD. Virgin rainforest north of Balikpapan near the eastern coast of Borneo has been clear-cut to allow for the continued planting of millions of acacia trees for pulp products and plywood.

(Left Middle) by UN Photo/WFP. Farmers harvest wheat in Badakhshan, Afghanistan. By improving grain storage facilities, a UN Food and Agriculture Organization project in Afghanistan reduced post-harvest losses from around 20 percent to less than 2 percent.

(Left Bottom) by Jakub Kozak. The city of Jaipur, India, has 3.3 million people. When the clearing of land for development compromised groundwater supplies, the city launched an ambitious urban greening program to reduce water runoff and recharge groundwater stores.

(Middle Top) 2006 IDEI, Courtesy of Photoshare. Women work on a small farm in Orissa, India.

(Middle Bottom) by Robert Corell. A fishing boat off the west coast of Greenland.

(Right Top) by UN Photo/Eskinder Debebe. A young girl in Kapisa Province, Afghanistan, in 2006.

(Right Middle) by Marco Flagg. A first grade art class at Guan Ai Primary School in Shanxi Province, China, a Rural China Education Foundation partner school. RCEF works with local teachers to develop creative curricula that promote independent thinking and civic engagement.

(Right Bottom) by UN Photo/Sean Sprague. Solar panels in Thies, Senegal.

Building a Sustainable and Desirable Economy-in-Society-in-Nature

Robert Costanza

Crawford School of Public Policy, The Australian National University

Gar Alperovitz

The Democracy Collaborative and Department of Government and Politics, University of Maryland

Herman Daly

School of Public Affairs, University of Maryland

Joshua Farley

Department of Community Development and Applied Economics, and Gund Institute for Ecological Economics, University of Vermont

Carol Franco

Woods Hole Research Center

Tim Jackson

Sustainable Lifestyles Research Group, University of Surrey

Ida Kubiszewski

Crawford School of Public Policy, The Australian National University

Juliet Schor

Department of Sociology, Boston College

and Peter Victor

Faculty of Environmental Studies, York University

Australian
National
University

E PRESS

Report to the United Nations for the 2012 Rio+20 Conference

as part of the Sustainable Development in the 21st Century (SD21) project implemented by the Division for Sustainable Development of the United Nations Department of Economic and Social Affairs

ANU
E PRESS

Published by ANU E Press
The Australian National University
Canberra ACT 0200, Australia
Email: anuepress@anu.edu.au
This title is also available online at http://epress.anu.edu.au

National Library of Australia Cataloguing-in-Publication entry

Author:	Constanza, Robert, author.
Title:	Building a sustainable and desirable economy-in-society-in-nature / Robert Constanza, Gar Alperovitz, Herman E. Daly, Joshua Farley, Carol Franco, Tim Jackson, Ida Kubiszewski, Juliet Schor, and Peter Victor.
ISBN:	9781921862045 (paperback) 9781921862052 (ebook)
Notes:	Includes bibliographical references.
Subjects:	Economic development--Environmental aspects. Environmental policy. Natural resources. Nature--Effect of human beings on.
Other Authors/Contributors:	Alperovitz, Gar, author. Daly, Herman E., author. Farley, Joshua, author. Franco, Carol, author. Jackson, Tim, author. Kubiszewski, Ida, author. Schor, Juliet, author. Victor, Peter A., 1946- author.
Dewey Number:	333.7

Cover design and layout by ANU E Press

Contents

Acknowledgements

This study is part of the Sustainable Development in the 21st Century (SD21) project. The project is implemented by the Division for Sustainable Development of the United Nations Department of Economic and Social Affairs, contract number 20465. Support from the European Commission is gratefully acknowledged.

This publication has been produced with the assistance of the European Union. The contents of this publication are the sole responsibility of the United Nations Department of Economic and Social Affairs and can in no way be taken to reflect the views of the European Union.

We thank David Le Blanc, project officer, for guidance and extremely useful feedback on earlier versions of this report. We also thank Ron Coleman and Thomas Prugh for editorial assistance. The ideas in this report have been published elsewhere by the authors and several sections are taken almost verbatim from these prior publications. Parts of the executive summary were crafted in direct discussions and consultations with the Royal Government of Bhutan in preparation of its draft outcome statement for its high-level meeting at the United Nations on 2nd April, 2012. The co-authors all agree on the general concepts and ideas but do not necessarily completely endorse every specific argument. This report is a synthesis and compendium.

Executive Summary

The world has changed dramatically. We no longer live in a world relatively empty of humans and their artifacts. We now live in the "Anthropocene," era [3] in a full world where humans are dramatically altering our ecological life-support system [4]. Our traditional economic concepts and models were developed in an empty world. If we are to create sustainable prosperity, if we seek "improved human well-being and social equity, while significantly reducing environmental risks and ecological scarcities," [5] we are going to need a new vision of the economy and its relationship to the rest of the world that is better adapted to the new conditions we face. We are going to need an economics that respects planetary boundaries [1,2], that recognizes the dependence of human well-being on social relations and fairness, and that recognizes that the ultimate goal is real, sustainable human well-being, not merely growth of material consumption. This new economics recognizes that the economy is embedded in a society and culture that are themselves embedded in an ecological life-support system [6-9], and that the economy cannot grow forever on this finite planet.

This report is a synthesis of ideas about what this new economy-in-society-in-nature could look like and how we might get there. Most of the ideas presented here are not new. The coauthors of this report have published them in various forms over the last several decades, and many others have expressed similar ideas in venues too numerous to mention. In particular, parts of this summary were crafted during discussions and consultations with the Royal Government of Bhutan in preparation of its draft outcome statement for its high-level meeting at the United Nations on 2nd April, 2012.

What is new is the timing and the situation. The time has come when we must make a transition. We have no choice. Our present path is clearly unsustainable. As Paul Raskin has said, "Contrary to the conventional wisdom, it is business as usual that is the utopian fantasy; forging a new vision is the pragmatic necessity." [10] But we do have a choice about how to make the transition and what the new state of the world will be. We can engage in a global dialogue to envision "the future we want," the theme of Rio+20, and then devise an adaptive strategy to get us there, or we can allow the current system to collapse and rebuild from a much worse starting point. We obviously argue for the former strategy.

In this report, we discuss the need to focus more directly on the goal of sustainable human well-being rather than merely GDP growth. This includes protecting and restoring nature, achieving social and intergenerational fairness (including poverty alleviation), stabilizing population, and recognizing the significant nonmarket contributions to human well-being from natural and social capital. To do this, we need to develop better measures of progress that go well beyond GDP and begin to measure human well-being and its sustainability more directly.

Our purpose in this report is to lay out a new model of the economy based on the worldview and principles of "ecological economics." [7-9] These include the ideas that:

1. our material economy is embedded in society, which is embedded in our ecological life-support system, and that we cannot understand or manage our economy without understanding the whole, interconnected system;

2. growth and development are not always linked and that true development must be defined in terms of the improvement of sustainable well-being (SWB), not merely improvement in material consumption; and

3. a healthy balance must be struck among thriving natural, human, social, and cultural assets, and adequate and well-functioning produced or built assets. We refer to these assets as "capital" in the sense of a stock or accumulation or heritage—a patrimony received from the past and contributing to the welfare of the present and future. Clearly our use of the term "capital" is much broader than that associated with capitalism.

These assets, which overlap and interact in complex ways to produce all human benefits, are defined as:

*   **Natural capital:** The natural environment and its biodiversity, which, in combination with the other three types of capital, provide ecosystem goods and services: the benefits humans derive from ecosystems. These goods and services are essential to basic needs such as survival, climate regulation, habitat for other species, water supply, food, fiber, fuel, recreation, cultural amenities, and the raw materials required for all economic production.

*   **Social and cultural capital:** The web of interpersonal connections, social networks, cultural heritage, traditional knowledge, trust, and the institutional arrangements, rules, norms, and values that facilitate human interactions and cooperation between people. These contribute to social cohesion to strong, vibrant, and secure communities, and to good governance, and help fulfil basic human needs such as participation, affection, and a sense of belonging.

*   **Human capital:** Human beings and their attributes, including physical and mental health, knowledge, and other capacities that enable people to be productive members of society. This involves the balanced use of time to meet basic human needs such as fulfilling employment, spirituality, understanding, skills development, creativity, and freedom.

*   **Built capital:** Buildings, machinery, transportation infrastructure, and all other human artifacts and services that fulfil basic human needs such as shelter, subsistence, mobility, and communications.

We recognise that human, social, and produced assets depend entirely on the natural world, and that natural capital is therefore ultimately non-substitutable. Sustainability thus requires that we live off the interest (sustainable yields) generated by natural capital without depleting the capital itself.

Balancing and investing in all the dimensions of our wealth to achieve sustainable well-being requires that:

1. we live within planetary boundaries—within the capacity of our finite planet to provide the resources needed for this and future generations;

2. that these resources are distributed fairly within this generation, between generations, and between humans and other species; and that

3. we use these finite resources as efficiently as possible to produce sustainable human well-being, recognizing its dependence on the well-being of the rest of nature.

We have never had greater global capacity, understanding, material abundance, and opportunities to achieve these objectives. This includes scientific knowledge, communications, technology, resources, productive potential, and ability to feed everyone on earth. However, we are not achieving sustainable well-being and indeed we are moving in the wrong direction at an increasing rate. For example, global greenhouse gas emissions continue to grow, humanity is using resources much faster than they can regenerate, biodiversity is diminishing rapidly, most global ecosystem services are in decline, and inequality is growing. The United Nations has acknowledged that progress towards the Millennium Development Goals has stalled.

"Business as usual" and continued movement in present directions threaten human survival on earth and is not an option. On a finite planet, excess consumption by high-income groups leaves less for lower-income groups and does not enhance human well-being. Many of these dangerous trends are a result of our current, unsustainable, growth-based economic paradigm, which rests on misused Gross Domestic Product (GDP)-based measures of progress. These measures largely ignore the value of natural and social capital and the distribution of wealth and income. They misleadingly count natural capital depletion and many human and social costs as economic gain. The architects of GDP themselves counseled that GDP should never be used as a measure of welfare, as it incorrectly is today. The European Union, the Organization for Economic Cooperation and Development, the Stiglitz Commission, and many others have therefore recognised the need to go beyond GDP.

We will never achieve the world we want unless we change the current economic paradigm, which is a fundamental cause of the current crises. This paradigm, institutionalized at Bretton Woods in 1944, was devised prior to an understanding of finite global resource limits or the emerging science of well-being. Without a new economic paradigm, we will continue down an unsustainable and undesirable path. Bretton Woods rightly considered a growth economy better than another World War, especially when the world was relatively empty. However, times have changed.

To make the transition to a just and sustainable world will require:

1. a fundamental change of worldview to one that recognises that we live on a finite planet and that sustainable well-being requires far more than material consumption;

2. replacing the present goal of limitless growth with goals of material sufficiency, equitable distribution, and sustainable human well-being; and

3. a complete redesign of the world economy that preserves natural systems essential to life and well-being and balances natural, social, human, and built assets.

The dimensions of the new economy include, but are not limited to, the following:

Sustainable scale: Respecting ecological limits

· Establishment of systems for effective and equitable governance and management of the natural commons, including the atmosphere, oceans, and biodiversity.

· Creation of cap-and-auction systems for basic resources, including quotas on depletion, pollution, and greenhouse gas emissions, based on basic planetary boundaries and resource limits.

· Consuming essential non-renewables, such as fossil fuels, no faster than we develop renewable substitutes.

- Investments in sustainable infrastructure, such as renewable energy, energy efficiency, public transit, watershed protection measures, green public spaces, and clean technology.
- Dismantling incentives towards materialistic consumption, including banning advertising to children and regulating the commercial media.
- Linked policies to address population and consumption.

Fair distribution: Protecting capabilities for flourishing

- Sharing the work to create more fulfilling employment and more balanced leisure-income trade-offs.
- Reducing systemic inequalities, both internationally and within nations, by improving the living standards of the poor, limiting excess and unearned income and consumption, and preventing private capture of common wealth.
- Establishment of a system for effective and equitable governance and management of the social commons, including cultural inheritance, financial systems, and information systems like the Internet and air waves.

Efficient allocation: Building a sustainable macro-economy

- Use of full-cost accounting measures to internalize externalities, value nonmarket assets and services, reform national accounting systems, and ensure that prices reflect actual social and environmental costs of production.
- Fiscal reforms that reward sustainable and well-being-enhancing actions and penalize unsustainable behaviours that diminish collective well-being, including ecological tax reforms with compensating mechanisms that prevent additional burdens on low-income groups.
- Systems of cooperative investment in stewardship (CIS) and payment for ecosystem services (PES).
- Increased financial and fiscal prudence, including greater public control of the money supply and its benefits and other financial instruments and practices that contribute to the public good.
- Ensuring availability of all information required to move to a sustainable economy that enhances well-being through public investment in research and development and reform of the ownership structure of copyrights and patents.

This report is largely targeted at the developed world in the emerging global full-world context. We chose this focus not because we think that the developing world is unimportant; quite the contrary. But we think that the policies we recommend can best be undertaken by the developed world, which needs to both create the ecological space for the developing world and set a good example of what real, human well-being-enhancing development can be.

This report contains some policy overlaps with recent UNEP (United Nations Environment Programme) and other reports on the "green economy" (GE), [5] but it differs significantly. GE reports assume that a green economy is still a growing economy in terms of GDP. In fact, they argue that a green economy can grow even faster than our current "brown economy." To do this, GDP would have to be significantly "decoupled" from material and fossil energy throughput. We believe that this decoupling should be encouraged to the extent possible, but that there are significant limits. The GE approach requires massive decoupling to achieve its results; our approach does not. The more decoupling the better, but we envision an economy that does not require it, and our policies actually incentivize it to the extent possible. We envision an economy where mere GDP growth is not the goal—an economy that can achieve truly sustainable human well-being with or without global GDP growth. What we do urgently need is reduction in material throughput that affects planetary boundaries. In addition, unlike the GE approach, we believe that a greatly expanded commons sector of the economy and new common asset institutions—not merely new markets for ecosystem services—are necessary to adequately deal with natural and social capital assets.

This report is divided into six sections.

Section 1 lays out why the current vision and system is not sustainable (it is exceeding planetary boundaries) and why it is also not desirable (it is not improving sustainable human well-being).

Section 2 briefly sketches a vision of what a sustainable and desirable economy-in-society-in-nature would look like in the year 2050. It covers the necessary changes in vision and worldview and the state of the world's built, human, social, and natural capital.

Section 3 looks at some of the policies necessary to achieve this vision, including those devoted to respecting ecological limits, building a sustainable macro-economy, and protecting capabilities for flourishing.

Section 4 goes into more detail on four of these policy reforms as examples. These cover reversing consumerism, expanding the commons, caps on natural resource use and pollution, and sharing the work.

Section 5 investigates evidence of whether these policies are consistent and feasible, by looking at historical examples, current small scale examples, and modeling studies.

Section 6 is a summary and conclusions.

We show in Section 5 that the policies we recommend are internally consistent and that the resulting system could be feasible, sustainable, and desirable. The substantial challenge is making the transition to this better world in a peaceful and positive way. There is no way to predict the exact path this transition might take, but we hope that painting this picture of a possible end-point and some milestones along the way will help make this choice and this journey a more viable option.

1. Rationale and Objectives

Key points:

- Growth in material consumption is unsustainable: there are fundamental planetary boundaries.
- Growth in material consumption beyond a threshold already reached by many is undesirable: it has negative effects on social and natural capital and in overdeveloped economies does not increase well-being.
- Viable alternatives exist that are both sustainable and desirable, but they require a fundamental redesign of the entire "regime."

The current mainstream model of the economy is based on a number of assumptions about the way the world works, what the economy is, and what the economy is for (Table 1). These assumptions arose in an earlier period. In this "empty-world" context, built capital was the limiting factor, while natural capital was abundant. It made sense, in that context, not to worry too much about environmental "externalities," since they could be assumed to be relatively small and ultimately solvable. It made sense to focus on the growth of the market economy, as measured by GDP, as a primary means to improve human welfare. It made sense, in that context, to think of the economy as only marketed goods and services and to think of the goal as increasing the amount of these goods and services produced and consumed.

But the world has changed dramatically. We now live in a world relatively full of humans and their built capital infrastructure. In this new context, we have to reconceptualize what the economy is and what it is for. We have to first remember that the goal of the economy should be to sustainably improve human well-being and quality of life. We have to remember that material consumption and GDP are merely means to that end, not ends in themselves. We have to recognize, as both ancient wisdom and new psychological research tell us, that too much of a focus on material consumption can actually reduce our well-being [11]. We have to better understand what really does contribute to sustainable human well-being (SHW) and recognize the substantial contributions of natural and social capital, which are now the limiting factors to improving SHW in many countries. We have to be able to distinguish between real poverty, in terms of low quality of life, and merely low monetary income. Ultimately we have to create a new vision of what the economy is and what it is for, and a new model of the economy that acknowledges this new "full-world" context and vision.

Some argue that relatively minor adjustments to the current economic model will produce the desired results. For example, they argue that by adequately pricing the depletion of natural capital (e.g., putting a price on carbon emissions) we can address many of the problems of the current economy while still allowing growth to continue. We call this approach the "green economy" (GE) model (Table 1). Some of the areas of intervention promoted by GE advocates, such as investing in natural capital. are necessary and we should pursue them. However, we do not agree that they are sufficient to achieve sustainable human well-being. We need a more fundamental change, a change of our goals and paradigm as discussed in the remainder of this report.

Table 1. Basic characteristics of the current economic model, the green economy model, and the ecological economics model [8].

	Current Economic Model	Green Economy Model	Ecological Economics Model
Primary policy goal	More: Economic growth in the conventional sense, as measured by GDP. The assumption is that growth will ultimately allow the solution of all other problems. More is always better.	More but with lower environmental impact: GDP growth decoupled from carbon and from other material and energy impacts.	Better: Focus must shift from merely growth to "development" in the real sense of improvement in sustainable human well-being, recognizing that growth has significant negative by-products. More is not always better.
Primary measure of progress	GDP.	Still GDP, but recognizing impacts on natural capital.	Index of Sustainable Economic Welfare (ISEW), Genuine Progress Indicator (GPI), or other improved measures of real welfare.
Scale/carrying capacity/role of environment	Not an issue, since markets are assumed to be able to overcome any resource limits via new technology, and substitutes for resources are always available.	Recognized, but assumed to be solvable via decoupling.	A primary concern as a determinant of ecological sustainability. Natural capital and ecosystem services are not infinitely substitutable and real limits exist.
Distribution/poverty	Given lip service, but relegated to "politics" and a "trickle-down" policy: a rising tide lifts all boats.	Recognized as important, assumes greening the economy will reduce poverty via enhanced agriculture and employment in green sectors.	A primary concern, since it directly affects quality of life and social capital and is often exacerbated by growth: a too rapidly rising tide only lifts yachts, while swamping small boats.
Economic efficiency/allocation	The primary concern, but generally including only marketed goods and services (GDP) and market institutions.	Recognized to include natural capital and the need to incorporate the value of natural capital into market incentives.	A primary concern, but including both market and nonmarket goods and services, and effects. Emphasis on the need to incorporate the value of natural and social capital to achieve true allocative efficiency.

	Current Economic Model	Green Economy Model	Ecological Economics Model
Property rights	Emphasis on private property and conventional markets.	Recognition of the need for instruments beyond the market.	Emphasis on a balance of property rights regimes appropriate to the nature and scale of the system, and a linking of rights with responsibilities. Includes larger role for common-property institutions in addition to private and state property.
Role of government	Government intervention to be minimized and replaced with private and market institutions.	Recognition of the need for government intervention to internalize natural capital.	Government plays a central role, including new functions as referee, facilitator, and broker in a new suite of common-asset institutions.
Principles of governance	Laissez-faire market capitalism.	ecognition of the need for government.	Lisbon principles of sustainable governance.

1.1. Some Background

The World Bank (WB) and the International Monetary Fund (IMF), founded at the Bretton Woods conference at the end of World War II, were chartered to speed economic development, stabilize the world economy, and end poverty. These institutions have relied largely on the current economic model as described above and in Table 1. The inability of these institutions and the later World Trade Organization (WTO), whose origins can also be traced to the Bretton Woods conference, to fully achieve their original goals of improving lives in the developing world and stabilizing the global economy has given rise to many critics, who are no longer marginalized voices of the displeased. These include former World Bank economists, the Group of 77 (G-77), and, increasingly, the millions of people in developed countries who have taken to the streets in protest. The policies under fire include removing barriers that check corporate access to a country's resources and often involve suspension of social and environmental legislation. Such policies can even over-ride national laws instituted through democratic processes. For example, the WTO once ruled that the United States Clean Air Act was a barrier to free trade. Such policies are antithetical to the goal of developing in a way that is sustainable, democratic, and equitable. They are also by no means agreed-upon in a broad consensus but are rather the dictates of a few powerful countries and their attendant organizations. Lending countries and their economists drove these policies, and borrowing nations have had little say in their implementation. Loans have required cuts in government salaries and privatization of social services. The conditional loans foisted upon many Latin American countries resulted in massive unemployment and devastating economic crises. In short, the execution of this model of the economy has led to unemployment, falling worker wages, biodiversity loss, environmental degradation, and disintegration of the social fabric.

Critics of the current model are many, and a coherent and viable alternative is sorely needed. Our purpose in this report is to lay out a new model of the economy based on the worldview and principles of ecological economics. [7-9] These include the ideas that:

1. our material economy is embedded in society which is embedded in our ecological life-support system, and that we cannot understand or manage our economy without understanding the whole, interconnected system;

2. growth and development are not always linked and that true development must be defined in terms of the improvement of sustainable human well-being, not merely improvement in material consumption; and

3. a balance of four basic types of assets (capital) are necessary for sustainable human well-being: built, human, social, and natural capital (financial capital is merely a marker for real capital and must be managed as such).

Before describing this new model, we provide a bit more background on why the current model is both unsustainable and undesirable.

1.2. Growth in Material Consumption is Unsustainable: There are Fundamental Planetary Boundaries

Historically, human recognition of our impact on the earth has consistently lagged behind the magnitude of the damage we have imposed, thus seriously weakening efforts to control this damage [12]. Even today, technological optimists and others ignore the mounting evidence of global environmental degradation, including climate disruption. Even some serious observers draw comfort from arguments such as the following:

· GDP figures are still increasing throughout much of the world.

· Life expectancies are still increasing in many nations.

· Evidence of human-caused climate disruption is still not absolutely definitive.

· Some claims of environmental damage have been exaggerated.

· Some previous predictions of environmental catastrophe have not been borne out.

Each of these statements is correct. However, not one of them is a reason for complacency, and indeed, taken together they should be viewed as powerful evidence of the need for an innovative approach. GDP and other current measures of national income accounting are notorious for overweighting market transactions, understating resource depletion, omitting pollution damage, and failing to measure real changes in well-being. For example, the Index of Sustainable Economic Welfare (ISEW), and a variation called the Genuine Progress Indicator (GPI), show significantly reduced improvement in real gains despite great increases in resource-depleting throughput. The ISEW and GPI also show increases in life expectancies in many nations, clearly indicating improvements in welfare; but unless accompanied by corresponding decreases in birth rates, such increases are warnings of acceleration in population growth, which will compound all other environmental problems. More details about these and other indicators of well-being are provided in section 1.3.

The pervasiveness of uncertainty about the basic nature of our ecological life-support systems and the recognition that complex systems often exhibit rapid, nonlinear changes and threshold effects emphasizes the need for building precautionary minimum safety standards into our policies [1].

Only relatively recently, with advances in environmental sciences, global remote sensing, and other monitoring systems, has a more comprehensive assessment of local and global environmental deterioration become possible. Evidence is accumulating with respect to accelerating loss of vital rain forests, species extinctions, depletion of ocean fisheries, shortages of freshwater in some areas and increased flooding in others, soil erosion, depletion and pollution of underground aquifers, decreases in quantity and quality of irrigation and drinking water, and growing global pollution of the atmosphere and oceans (even in the polar regions), including global climate disruption by carbon dioxide enrichment and other greenhouse gases [1,13]. Obviously the exponential growth of human populations, recently surpassing 7 billion, is rapidly crowding out other species before we have begun to understand fully our dependence on species diversity.

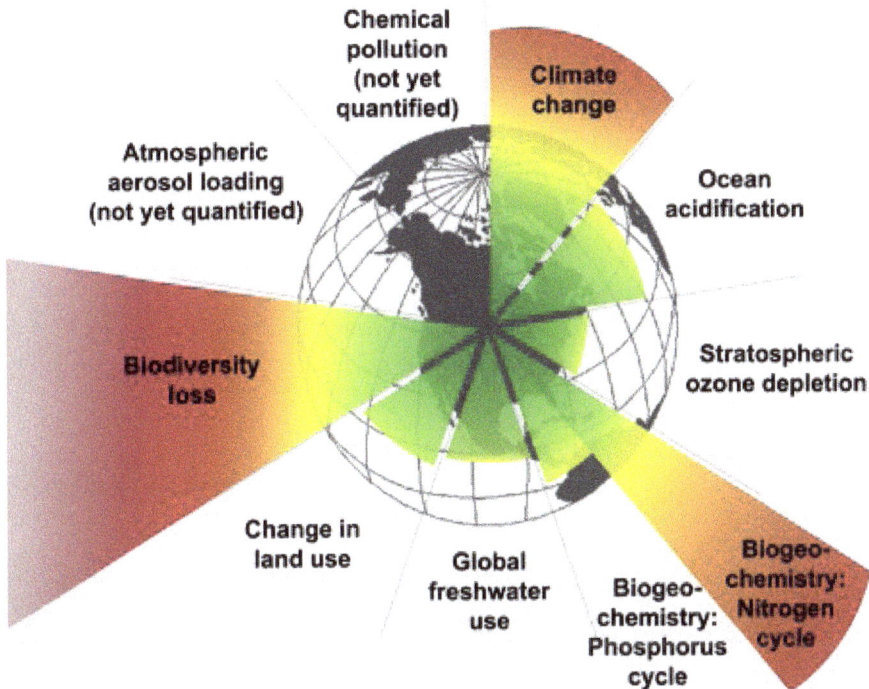

Figure 1. Planetary boundaries [1,2].

Even more fundamentally, our planet's ability to provide an accommodating environment for humanity itself is being challenged by our own activities. The environment—our life-support system—is changing rapidly from the stable Holocene state of the last 12,000 years, during which we developed agriculture, villages, cities, and contemporary civilizations, to an unknown future state of significantly different conditions. We have entered what Paul Crutzen [3] has identified as a whole new geologic era—the Anthropocene.

One way to address this challenge is to determine "safe boundaries" based on fundamental characteristics of our planet and to operate within them. "Boundaries" here mean specific points related to a global-scale environmental process beyond which humanity should not go. Identifying our planet's intrinsic, nonnegotiable limits is not easy, but recently a team of scientists has specified nine areas that are most in need of well-defined planetary boundaries [1]. These nine areas are (1) climate change, (2) biodiversity loss, (3) excess nitrogen and phosphorus production, (4) stratospheric ozone depletion, (5) ocean acidification, (6) global consumption of freshwater, (7) change in land use for agriculture, (8) air pollution, and (9) chemical pollution (Figure 1). Rockström and colleagues estimate that humanity has already transgressed three of these boundaries: climate change, biodiversity loss, and nitrogen production, with several others rapidly approaching the safe boundary.

Clearly, remedial policy responses to date have been local, partial, and inadequate. Early policy discussions and the resulting responses tended to focus on symptoms of environmental damage rather than basic causes, and policy instruments tend to be ad hoc rather than carefully designed for efficiency, fairness, and sustainability. For example, in the 1970s emphasis centered on end-of-pipe pollution which, while a serious problem, was actually a symptom of expanding populations and inefficient technologies that fueled exponential growth of material and energy throughput while threatening the recuperative powers of the planet's life-support systems.

As a result of early perceptions of environmental damage, people learned a lot about policies and instruments for attacking pollution. These insights will help in dealing with the more fundamental and intractable environmental issues identified here.

The basic problems for which we need innovative policies and management instruments include:

- unsustainably large and growing human populations, as well as growing per capita consumption levels that are fast approaching, or already exceed, planetary boundaries;

- highly entropy-increasing technologies that deplete the earth of its resources and whose unassimilated wastes poison the air, water, and land; and

- land conversion that destroys habitat, increases soil erosion, and accelerates loss of species diversity, and which, coupled with resource extraction and waste emissions, decreases the ecosystem services that support humanity.

These problems are all evidence that the material scale of human activity is rapidly approaching, or already exceeds, the safe operating space for humanity on the earth.

We argue throughout this report that in addressing these problems we should adopt courses of action based on:

- recognition of the planetary boundaries the earth places on the type and scale of economic activity;

- fair distribution of resources and opportunities among groups within the present generation, between present and future generations, and between humans and other species; and

- economically efficient[1] allocation of resources that adequately accounts for protecting the stocks of natural and social capital.

Homo sapiens is at another turning point in its relatively long and (so far) inordinately successful history. Our species' activities on the planet have now reached such a scale that they are beginning to affect the ecological life-support system itself. The entire concept of economic growth (defined as increasing material consumption) must be rethought, especially as a solution to the growing host of interrelated social, economic, and environmental problems. What we need now is real economic and social development (qualitative improvement without growth in resource throughput) and an explicit recognition of the interrelatedness and interdependence of all aspects of life on the planet. We need to move from an economics that ignores this interdependence to one that acknowledges and builds on it. We need to develop an economics that is fundamentally "ecological" in the broadest sense and in its basic view of the problems that our species currently faces.

1.3. Growth in Material Consumption Beyond a Certain Point is Undesirable: It has Negative Effects on Well-Being and on Social and Natural Capital

There is a substantial body of new research on what actually contributes to human well-being and quality of life. While there is still much ongoing debate, this new science clearly demonstrates the limits of conventional economic income and consumption in contributing to well-being. For example, psychologist Tim Kasser, in his 2003 book *The High Price of Materialism* [11], points out that people who focus on material consumption as a path to well-being are actually less satisfied with their lives and even suffer higher rates of both physical and mental illness than those who do not focus so much on material consumption. Material consumption beyond real need is a form of psychological "junk food" that only satisfies for the moment and ultimately leads to depression, Kasser says.

Economist Richard Easterlin has shown that well-being tends to correlate well with health, level of education, and marital status and shows sharply diminishing returns to income beyond a fairly low threshold. He concludes [14] that

> people make decisions assuming that more income, comfort, and positional goods will make them happier, failing to recognize that hedonic adaptation and social comparison will come into play, raise their aspirations to about the same extent as their actual gains, and leave them feeling no happier than before. As a result, most individuals spend a disproportionate amount of their lives working to make money, and sacrifice family life and health, domains in which aspirations remain fairly constant as actual circumstances change, and where the attainment of one's goals has a more lasting impact on happiness. Hence, a reallocation of time in favor of family life and health would, on average, increase individual happiness.

---

1 "Economically efficient" simply means that increasing marginal costs and diminishing marginal benefits from an activity are in balance. Marginal costs and benefits should be measured in terms of contributions to the sustainable welfare of humans and other species. Precise measurement of these contributions is not currently possible. Conventional economists emphasize purely monetary costs and benefits, which are determined by willingness to pay, and hence fail to reflect costs and benefits for those with limited purchasing power. Under these conditions, an efficient allocation is one that maximizes monetary value. While measurements may be fairly precise, this narrow goal is inappropriate.

British economist Richard Layard synthesizes many of these ideas and concludes that current economic policies are not improving well-being and happiness and that "happiness should become the goal of policy, and the progress of national happiness should be measured and analyzed as closely as the growth of GNP [gross national product]." [15]

Economist Robert Frank, in his book *Luxury Fever* [16], also concludes that some nations would be better off—that is, overall national well-being would be higher—if we actually consumed less and spent more time with family and friends, working for our communities, maintaining our physical and mental health, and enjoying nature.

On this last point, there is substantial and growing evidence that natural systems contribute heavily to human well-being. In a paper published in the journal *Nature* [8], the annual, nonmarket value of the earth's ecosystem services was estimated to be substantially larger than global GDP. This estimate was admittedly a rough first cut, but the goal of this paper was to stimulate interest and research on the topic of natural capital and ecosystem services. It has certainly had that effect. The paper is one of the most highly cited in the ecology/environment area in the last 15 years and it has stimulated a huge amount of discussion, research, and policy follow-up. For example, the UN Millennium Ecosystem Assessment [17] was a global update and compendium of ecosystem services and their contributions to human well-being. The Economics of Ecosystems and Biodiversity (TEEB) Synthesis report [18] is a more recent contribution to this rapidly increasing field of study and policy. The World Bank has recently announced itsd Wealth Accounting and Valuation of Ecosystem Services (WAVES) project. The new Intergovernmental Platform on Biodiversity and Ecosystem Services (IPBES) is also in the formation stages (http://www.ipbes.net). Finally, the recently established Ecosystem Services Partnership (ESP) is a global effort to coordinate the thousands of researchers and practitioners around this topic (http://www.es-partnership.org).

So, if we want to assess the "real" economy—all the things that contribute to real, sustainable, human well-being—as opposed to only the "market" economy, we have to measure and include the non-marketed contributions to human well-being from nature; from family, friends, and other social relationships at many scales; and from health and education. What does such a more comprehensive, integrative definition of well-being and quality of life look like?

1.3.1. An integrative definition of quality of life and well-being[2]

When we evaluate the state of human affairs or propose policies to improve it, we typically proceed from assumptions about the characteristics of a good life and strategies for achieving them. We might suppose, for example, that access to particular resources is a part of a good life and, therefore, that increasing economic production per-capita is an appropriate goal. Unfortunately, our underlying assumptions are rarely tested and established. We therefore need a more basic approach to defining well-being or quality of life (QOL) that, in turn, can guide our efforts to improve humans' experience. Examinations of QOL often fall under two headings:

1. So-called "objective" indicators of QOL include, for example, indices of economic production (i.e., GDP), literacy rates, life expectancy, and other data that can

---

2 Much of this section is taken from reference 19. Costanza R, Fisher B, Ali S, Beer C, Bond L, et al. (2007) Quality of life: An approach integrating opportunities, human needs, and subjective well-being. Ecological Economics 61: 267-276.

be gathered without a subjective evaluation being made by the individual being assessed (although, of course, we must acknowledge that subjective judgments of the researcher are involved in the process of defining and gathering "objective" measures as seen in the case, for example, of selecting a proxy for "literacy"). Objective indicators may be used singly or in combination to form summary indexes, as in the UN's Human Development Index (HDI) [20], the Index of Sustainable Economic Welfare , or Genuine Progress Indicator. To the extent that such a measure can be shown to be valid and reliable across assessment contexts (admittedly a difficult task), these relatively objective measures may help us gather standardized data that are less vulnerable to social comparison and local adaptation. For example, a valid measure should minimize the degree to which QOL is largely a function of comparing one's life to others' in one's locale, in the media, or some other narrowly construed group; a person's QOL should not be considered high simply because others in the locale are more miserable.

2. Subjective indicators of QOL gain their impetus, in part, from the observation that many objective indicators merely assess the opportunities that individuals have to improve QOL rather than assessing QOL itself. Thus economic production may best be seen as a *means* to a potentially (but not necessarily) improved QOL rather than an end in itself. In addition, unlike most objective measures of QOL, subjective measures typically rely on survey or interview tools to gather respondents' own assessments of their lived experiences in the form of self-reports of satisfaction, happiness, well-being, or some other near-synonym. Rather than presume the importance of various life domains (e.g., life expectancy or material goods), subjective measures can also tap the perceived significance of the domain (or "need") to the respondent. Diener and Suh provide convincing evidence that subjective indicators are valid measures of what people perceive to be important to their happiness and well-being [21]. Nevertheless, there are individuals who cannot provide subjective reports or whose subjective reports may not be as trustworthy in reflecting their true welfare because of the internalization of cultural norms [22], mental illness, lack of information, or other reasons.

What seems best, then, is to attempt an approach to QOL that combines objective and subjective approaches. Our integrative definition of QOL is as follows: QOL is the extent to which objective human needs are fulfilled in relation to personal or group perceptions of subjective well-being (Figure 2). Human needs are basic needs for subsistence, reproduction, security, affection, etc. (see Table 1 and below). SWB is assessed by individuals' or groups' responses to questions about happiness, life satisfaction, utility, or welfare. The relation between specific human needs and perceived satisfaction with each of them can be affected by mental capacity, cultural context, information, education, temperament, and the like, often in quite complex ways. Moreover, the relation between the fulfillment of human needs and overall subjective well-being is affected by the (time-varying) weights individuals, groups, and cultures give to fulfilling each of the human needs relative to the others.

With this definition, the role of policy is to create opportunities for human needs to be met, understanding that there exists a diversity of ways to meet any particular need. Built, human, social, and natural capitals represent one way of categorizing those opportunities. Time is also an independent constraint on the achievement of human needs.

Social norms affect both the weights given to various human needs when aggregating them to overall individual or social assessments of SWB, and also policy decisions about social investments in improving opportunities. Social norms evolve over time due to collective population behavior [24]. The evolution of social norms can be affected by conscious shared envisioning of preferred states of the world [25].

As we said, one convenient way to summarize the opportunities for meeting human needs is to group them into four basic types of assets or "capital" that are necessary to support the real, human-well-being-producing economy: built capital, human capital, social capital, and natural capital.

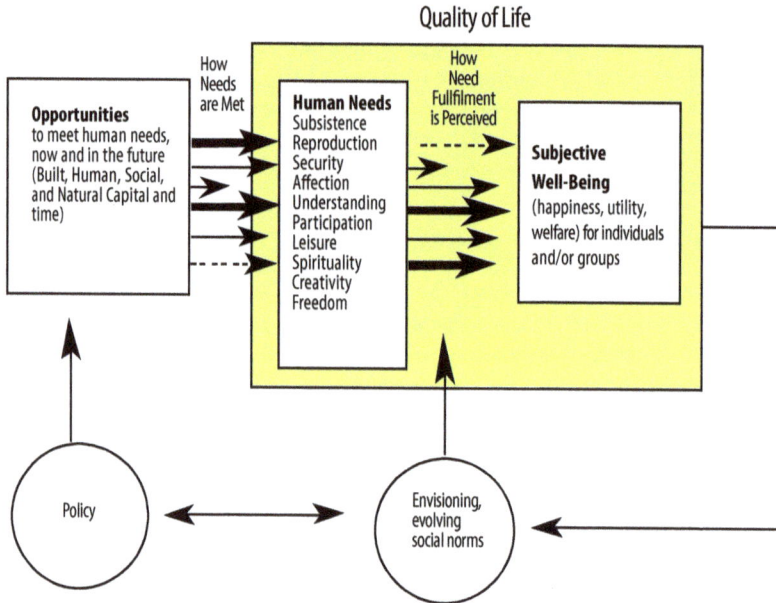

Figure 2. Quality of Life (QOL) as the interaction of human needs and the subjective perception of their fulfillment, as mediated by the opportunities available to meet the needs [23].

We refer to these assets as "capital" in the sense of a stock or accumulation or heritage—a patrimony received from the past and contributing to the welfare of the present and future. Clearly our use of the term "capital" is much broader than that associated with capitalism. These assets, which overlap and interact in complex ways to produce all benefits, are generally defined as follows:

- **Natural capital:** The natural environment and its biodiversity. Among other things, natural capital is needed to provide ecosystem goods and services. These goods and services are essential to basic human needs such as survival, climate regulation, habitat for other species, water supply, food, fiber, fuel, recreation, cultural amenities, and the raw materials required for all economic production.

- **Social and cultural capital:** The web of interpersonal connections, social networks, cultural heritage, traditional knowledge, and trust, and the institutional arrangements, rules, norms, and values that facilitate human interactions and cooperation between people. These contribute to social cohesion; strong, vibrant, and secure communities; and good governance, and help fulfill basic human needs such as participation, affection, and a sense of belonging.

- **Human capital:** Human beings and their attributes, including physical and mental health, knowledge, and other capacities that enable people to be productive members of society. This involves the balanced use of time to fulfill basic human needs such as satisfying employment, spirituality, understanding, skills development, creativity, and freedom.
- **Built capital:** Buildings, machinery, transportation infrastructure, and all other human artifacts and services that fulfill basic human needs such as shelter, subsistence, mobility, and communications.

We recognise that human, social, and produced assets depend entirely on the natural world, and that natural capital is therefore ultimately non-substitutable. Sustainability therefore requires that we live off the interest (sustainable yields) generated by natural capital without depleting the capital itself.

To think of nature, the biosphere, the earth as a form of capital is a way of recognizing its importance to the economy, an importance that is often overlooked. Ecological economics understands economies as embedded in cultures and societies, which are embedded in the geobiosphere. This means that economies rely on the geobiosphere to provide materials and energy and accommodate all the wastes that economic activity inevitably produces. Natural capital is similar to built capital (buildings, machines, infrastructure, warehouses) in that it provides goods (e.g., minerals, fossil fuels) and services (e.g., pollination, flood control) without which economies could not function.

In speaking of "natural capital" we are using the term "capital" in its physical, not financial sense, e.g., a carpenter's stock of tools or a factory assembly line. A herd of livestock is a capital stock that yields a flow of new members. The physical herd converts grass, water, etc., into new animals. The net increment is income or sustainable yield. The constant herd is capital, reproducing stock. This is a physical stock-flow relation independent of financial arrangements. Indeed the word "capital" derives from "capitas," the number of heads the herdsman has in his live stock. Similar stock-flow relationships hold for forests, fisheries, and other populations. The problems arise when the physical descriptive term "natural capital" is converted into financial monetary terms, and especially when natural growth rates are converted into monetary yields of different physical stocks, and then compared to the rate of interest on a stock of money in the bank. But reasonable rejection of financialization of nature should not keep us from recognizing the physical importance of natural capital as a stock that yields desired flows.

But natural capital is also very different from built capital. First of all, built capital is made from natural capital. In other words, nature can exist without built capital, but built capital cannot exist without nature. There is an essential hierarchy limiting the extent to which built capital can substitute for natural capital, and they are better thought of complements than substitutes.

Second, built capital represents a "fund" that provides a "service," as, for example, a lathe provides a service when it is used to shape wood. The lathe does not end up embodied in the wood. Natural capital can also be a fund that provides services, such as when a forest provides habitat for forest creatures. But natural capital can also be a stock out of which a supply of material flows. So the forest that provides habitat as a fund-service is also a stock of trees that supplies a flow of wood (the very wood used on the lathe.) Services do not deplete funds. Flows do deplete stocks, which can however be regenerated if renewable. Since materials flowing from natural capital are usually sold through markets, and ecosystem services often are not, there is an ever-present tendency to overuse natural capital for the flows it can provide to the detriment of its capacity to provide services.

A third and more profound reason for differentiating between natural and built capital is that built capital is simply an object for the benefit of humans. That is why it exists. When built capital no long provides a useful service, it is demolished. Nature, of which humans are an integral part, is much more than that. Nature is populated by countless species, many of whom are sentient, experience a range of emotions, learn, and live in communities of their own making. Reverence for all life acknowledges that the rest of nature has rights and that a fair distribution of resources needs to acknowledge those rights. Thus, thinking of built capital and natural capital as substitutes is not appropriate, as a common designation of both of them as forms of capital might otherwise suggest.

With these caveats in mind, we employ the concept of natural capital in this report cognizant of its limitations [26].

1.3.2. Are we making progress?

Given this definition of well-being and quality of life, are we really making progress? Is the mainstream economic model really working, even in the developed countries? One way to tell is through surveys of people's life satisfaction, which have been relatively flat in the United States and many other developed countries since about 1975, in spite of a near doubling in per capita income (Figure 3).

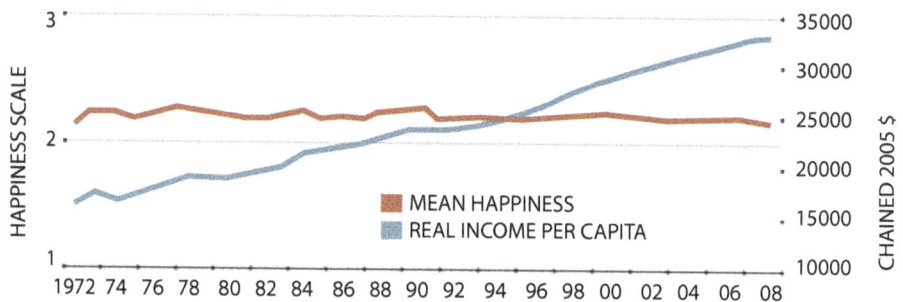

Figure 3. Happiness and Real Income in the United States, 1972–2008. NOTE: Mean happiness (left scale) is the average reply from respondents to the U.S. General Social Survey. The survey question asks: "Taken all together, how would you say things are these days? Would you say that you are not too happy, pretty happy or very happy?" These values were coded as 1, 2 and 3, respectively [27].

A second approach is an aggregate measure of the real economy that has been developed as an alternative to GDP called the Index of Sustainable Economic Well-Being (ISEW) or a variation called the Genuine Progress Indicator(GPI).

Let's first take a quick look at the problems with GDP as a measure of true human well-being. GDP is not only limited—measuring only marketed economic activity or gross income—it also counts all of this activity as positive. It does not separate desirable, well-being-enhancing activity from undesirable, well-being-reducing activity. For example, an oil spill increases GDP because someone has to clean it up, but it obviously detracts from society's well-being. From the perspective of GDP, more crime, more sickness, more war, more pollution, more fires, storms, and pestilence are all potentially good things, because they can increase marketed activity in the economy.

GDP also leaves out many things that *do* enhance well-being but are outside the market. For example, the unpaid work of parents caring for their own children at home does not show up; but if these same parents decide to work outside the home to pay for childcare, GDP suddenly increases. The nonmarketed work of natural capital in providing clean air and water, food, natural resources, and other ecosystem services does not adequately show up in GDP either; but if those services are damaged and we have to pay to fix or replace them, then GDP suddenly increases. Finally, GDP takes no account of the distribution of income among individuals. But it is well known that an additional dollar of income produces more well-being if one is poor rather than rich. In fact, GDP is maximized by allocating resources to those with the greatest willingness to pay. In a highly unequal society, a rich person may be willing to pay more for drinking water to flush their toilets than a poor family can pay to prevent a child from dying of dysentery. It is also clear that a highly skewed income distribution has negative effects on a society's social capital.

The GPI addresses these problems by separating the positive from the negative components of marketed economic activity, adding in estimates of the value of nonmarketed goods and services provided by natural, human, and social capital, and adjusting for income-distribution effects. While the measure is by no means a perfect representation of the real well-being of nations, GPI is a much better approximation than GDP. As many have noted, it is much better to be approximately right in these measures than precisely wrong.

Comparing GDP and GPI for the United States (Figure 4) shows that, while GDP has steadily increased since 1950, with the occasional dip or recession, GPI peaked in about 1975 and has been flat or gradually decreasing ever since. From the perspective of the real economy, as opposed to just the market economy, the United States has been in recession since 1975. As already mentioned, this picture is also consistent with survey-based research on people's stated life-satisfaction. The United States and several other developed countries are now in a period of what Herman Daly has called "uneconomic growth," where further growth in marketed economic activity (GDP) is actually reducing well-being, on balance, rather than enhancing it. In terms of the four capitals, while built and some aspects of human capital have grown, social and natural capital have declined or remained constant, more than canceling out the gains in built and human capital.

GPI is certainly not the perfect indicator of well-being or quality of life (QOL) and there are several other alternatives under active discussion [28,29]. As we discussed earlier, QOL is a complex interaction of objective and subjective factors and the relationships among them, and sustainable human well-being is an active area of research. Nevertheless, GPI is certainly a better approximation to the objective elements of well-being than GDP, a function for which GDP was never designed. In addition, GPI data for the United States and other countries seem to match subjective well-being surveys much better than income or GDP data.

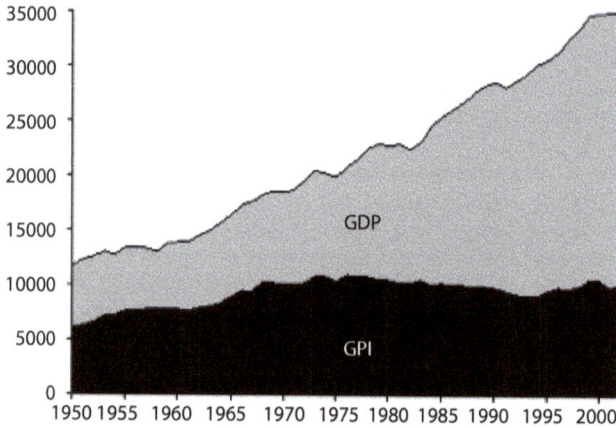

Figure 4. GDP (Gross Domestic Product) and GPI (Genuine Progress Indicator) for the U.S. from 1950 to 2005 [30].

1.4. Viable Alternatives Exist that are Both Sustainable and Desirable, but they Require a Fundamental Redesign of the Entire "Regime"

A new model of the economy consistent with our new full-world context (Table 1) would be based clearly on the goal of sustainable human well-being. It would use measures of progress that clearly acknowledge this goal (e.g., GPI instead of GDP). It would acknowledge the importance of ecological sustainability, social fairness, and real economic efficiency.

Ecological sustainability implies recognizing that natural and social capitals are not infinitely substitutable by built and human capital and that real biophysical limits and planetary boundaries exist to the expansion of the market economy. Climate change is perhaps the most obvious and compelling of these limits.

Social fairness implies recognizing that the distribution of wealth is an important determinant of social capital and quality of life. The conventional economic model, while explicitly aimed at reducing poverty, has bought into the assumption that the best way to do this is through growth in GDP. This has not proved to be the case, and explicit attention to distribution issues is sorely needed. As Robert Frank has argued [31], economic growth beyond a certain point sets up a "positional arms race" that changes the consumption context and forces everyone to consume too much of positional goods (like houses and cars) at the expense of nonmarketed, nonpositional goods and services from natural and social capital. Increasing inequality of income actually reduces overall societal well-being, not just for the poor but across the income spectrum. Wilkinson and Pickett [32] have produced empirical data that show a strong correlation between income inequality in OECD countries and a whole range of health and social problems. Large income inequality is as detrimental to the well-being of the rich as to the poor.

Real economic efficiency implies including all resources that affect sustainable human well-being in the allocation and management system. Our current market-focused allocation system excludes most non-marketed natural and social capital assets and services that are huge contributors to human well-being. The current economic model ignores this and therefore does not achieve real economic efficiency. A new, sustainable model would measure and include the contributions of natural and social capital in ways that go well beyond the market. This would better approximate real economic efficiency.

The new model would also acknowledge that a complex set of property rights regimes is necessary to adequately manage the full range of resources that contribute to human well-being. For example, most natural and social capital assets are part of the commons. Making them private property does not work well. When a resource is non-rival (meaning that use by one person does not leave less for others to use), then market prices will ration access to those who can afford to pay, even though additional use incurs no additional costs. The clearest example of this is information. In fact, for information that protects the environment or provides other social benefits—for example, an inexpensive, carbon-free energy technology—additional use actually reduces social costs. The value of such resources is paradoxically maximized at a price of zero (or less). Since the private sector will not provide products for free, the public sector must be responsible for their protection and provision. On the other hand, when resources are rival, meaning that use by one person leaves less for others, leaving them as open-access resources (with no property rights) does not work well either. What is needed is a third way to *propertize* these resources without privatizing them. Several new (and old) common-property-rights systems have been proposed to achieve this goal, including various forms of common-property trusts. These are described in detail later in this report.

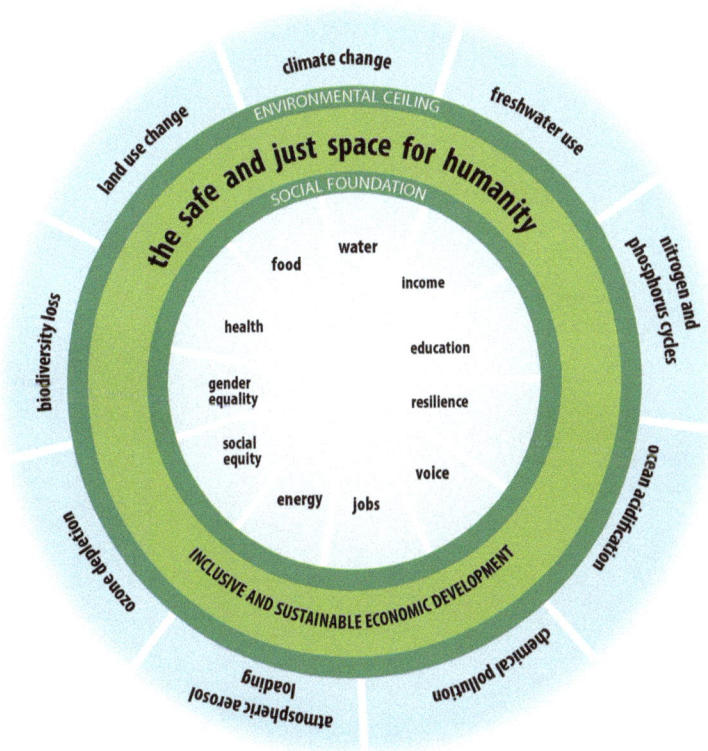

Figure 5. A safe and just space for humanity - the sustainable and desirable doughnut [36].

The role of government also needs to be reinvented. In addition to government's role in regulating and policing the private market economy, it has a significant role to play in expanding the commons sector, which can propertize and manage non-marketed natural and social capital assets. It can also help develop new common-ownership models at various levels of scale that are not driven by growth principles, and can play a planning and coordinating role to help manage a reduced-growth regime [33]. Government also has a major role to play in facilitating societal development of a shared vision of what a sustainable and desirable future would look like. As Tom Prugh and colleagues [34] have argued, a strong democracy, based on developing a shared vision, is an essential prerequisite to building a sustainable and desirable future.

One way to look at our goals for the new economy is shown in (Figure 5). This figure combines planetary boundaries (Figure 1) as the "environmental ceiling" with basic human needs (Figure 2) as the "social foundation" [35]. This creates an environmentally sustainable and socially desirable and just "doughnut" as the space within which humanity can thrive.

In the remainder of this report we more fully develop these ideas, beginning with a vision of what such a sustainable and desirable society living within the doughnut could look like.

2. What Would a Sustainable and Desirable Economy-in-Society-in-Nature Look Like?

Key point:

• To better articulate and communicate the goal, we need to envision the resulting society and how the pieces might fit together.

The most critical task facing humanity today is the creation of a shared vision of a sustainable and desirable society, one that can provide permanent prosperity within the biophysical constraints of the real world in a way that is fair and equitable to all of humanity, to other species, and to future generations. Recent work with businesses and communities indicates that creating a shared vision is the most effective engine for change in the desired direction [37].

In the previous sections we have sketched out the general characteristics of this world and how it differs from our current society: it is ecologically sustainable, fair, efficient, and secure. Here we put all the policies together and develop the implications for the whole system. We need to fill in the details in a coherent vision that is tangible enough to motivate all kinds of people to work toward achieving it. Without a coherent, relatively detailed, shared vision of what a sustainable society could look like, there will be no political will nor united effort to take us from here to there. The default vision of continued, unlimited increases in material consumption is inherently unsustainable and undesirable, as we have pointed out, but we cannot break away from this vision until a credible and widely shared alternative is created.

Below we sketch out one version of such a vision as a starting point.[1] There are several other visioning exercises that have created similar descriptions, including the Great Transition Initiative (http://www.gtinitiative.org) and the Future We Want (http://www.futurewewant.org). Ultimately, this vision must be shared and further developed through participatory democratic processes.

If humanity is to achieve a sustainable and desirable future, we must create a shared vision detailing what we as a society want to sustain and incorporating the central shared values that express our hopes for the future. This vision must incorporate a diversity of perspectives and be based on principles of fairness, respect, and sustainability.

This draft vision is divided into five parts: (1) worldviews, (2) built capital, (3) human capital, (4) social capital, and (5) natural capital, encompassing the basic elements of the

---

1 This vision is adapted from one created at a workshop held at Oberlin College in January 2001, attended by the following: Audra Abt, Gar Alperovitz, Mary Barber, Seaton Baxter, Janine Benyus, Paul W. Bierman-Lytle, Grace Boggs, William Browning, Diana Bustamante, Warren W. Byrne, Mark Clevey, Jane Ellen Clougherty, Robert Costanza, Tanya Dawkins, James Embry, Jon Farley, Joshua Farley, Harold Glasser, Becky Grella, Elaine Gross, Gerald Hairston, Sarah Karpanty, Carol Kuhre, George McQuitty, Peter Montague, Dondohn Namesling, Aiza Biby, David Orr, John Petersen, William Prindle, Tom Prugh, Jack Santa-Barbara, Claudine Schneider, Ben Shepherd, Megan Snedden, Karl Steyaert, Theodore Steck, Harvey Stone, Paul Templet, Mary Evelyn Tucker, Sarah van Gelder, Rafael Vargas, and Verlene Wilder.

ecological economics framework. This vision is written from the perspective of the year 2050, describing the world we have achieved by implementing the policies outlined in previous sections.

2.1. Worldview

Our worldview no longer divides the planet into "humans vs. nature." People now recognize that humans are a part of nature, one species among many, and must obey the laws and constraints imposed on all of nature. Nevertheless, humans bear responsibility that other creatures do not—we don't blame deer for overgrazing—yet we expect humans to recognize their "overgrazing" and stop it. We recognize that nature is not something to be subjugated, but instead is something we depend upon absolutely to meet physical, psychological, cultural, and spiritual needs. We recognize that natural resources are scarce and must be invested in. Our goal is to create conditions conducive to life in the broadest sense.

For centuries the worldview of mechanistic physics dominated Western society. Within this worldview, each action has an equal and opposite reaction, and only by studying systems at smaller and smaller scales can we come to fully understand these reactions. As more and more people have come to understand the inherent complexity of ecosystems and human systems, we have come to realize that results cannot always be predicted and that irreducible uncertainty dominates the provision of life-support services by healthy ecosystems.

An ecological worldview of complexity and indeterminacy, inspired by nature as mentor—holistic, integrated, and flexible—has replaced the worldview of mechanistic physics. Unfettered individualism is appropriate and even necessary in a world of vast frontiers and unlimited elbow room. Individualism is still extremely important in 2050, but is far more tempered by a concern for the common good. This has led to a system where communities promote individual liberty as long as individual actions do not have a negative impact on the community. Individuals in return accept that they are a part of society, and it is unfair and illegal (even uneconomic) to impose costs on society for private gain. This attitude was necessary to wean ourselves of our dependence on heavily polluting single-occupancy vehicles, for example.

Further, ever-increasing consumption is no longer considered an integral component of human needs as it was in the early part of the century. People pay attention to their other needs and desires, such as joy, beauty, affection, participation, creativity, freedom, and understanding. Building strong community helps us meet these needs, while working ever harder to pay for more consumption deprives us of the time and energy required to fulfill them. Thus, status is not conferred by high incomes and high consumption (individual ends), but rather by contribution to civil society and community ends. With the recognition that consumption beyond limit is not only physically unsustainable but also does little to improve our quality of life, we now understand that a "steady-state" economy—prosperous but within planetary boundaries—is our goal. A steady-state economy does not mean an end to development; it simply means that we limit the input of raw materials into our economic system and their inevitable return to the ecosystem as waste to a level compatible with the ecological constraints imposed by a finite planet with finite resources. We now live happily and well within the safe operating space of our planet. We do not know the precise location of these planetary boundaries, and they are subject to change. Therefore, "adaptive management" has become the guiding principle.

The economy is now powered by our incoming solar energy—direct sunlight captured by solar panels—as well as wind, hydro, and the traditional forms of solar energy capture (agriculture, forestry, and fisheries). Economic production now focuses on quality, not quantity, on everyone having enough, and on fulfilling employment. Rather than the earlier focus on the production of goods, we now focus on the production of the services provided by goods and how those services are distributed. We do not need cars, we need transportation. We do not need televisions, we need entertainment and information. Goods are only a means to an end—the larger end of sustainable human well-being— and by recognizing this our economy has developed as never before without growing in physical terms.

2.2. Built Capital

Built capital is the human-made infrastructure used to meet human needs. Technological advance over the last century has had a large impact on the type of built capital we find in 2050. Different priorities have had as much or even greater impact.

Housing: Communities have been dramatically redesigned to integrate living space, community space, and workspace with recreational needs and nature. Workspace includes the stores that supply our everyday needs as well as production facilities for most of the goods those stores supply. People now live very close to where they work, where they shop, and where they play. The huge cities of the early twenty-first century did not disappear, but they have been dramatically reorganized. Cities are now aggregations of smaller communities in close physical proximity but where each community meets the housing, employment, social, recreation, and shopping needs of those who live there. The "20-minute neighborhood" idea—that all basic services should be no more than a 20-minute walk away—has taken hold as an urban design principle. Natural areas have also made a big comeback in cities. The specifics of community size and design are, of course, determined by local physical and cultural conditions, and there is enormous diversity.

In addition to these very practical aspects, communities have been designed as soul-satisfying spaces that resonate with our evolutionary history. Most communities include natural areas and incorporate parks and other green spaces (though "green" is a misnomer in drier parts of the world, where xeriscaping is the norm), and such spaces also serve as common space for community members. They also foster social interaction and community. Rather than something new, this is simply a resurgence of a millennial tradition of settlement patterns.

Because community space is abundant and well designed, private homes are generally smaller (hence cheaper and easier to care for) and are much more energy efficient. Private lawns have virtually disappeared, though lawn-like community green spaces still exist, and private gardens abound. Private gardens in fact meet a substantial portion of community food needs. Walking and bicycle riding have effectively become the dominant forms of transportation, except in the worst weather. Rapidly increasing energy costs provided the initial incentive, but people then discovered the enormous benefits of such pedestrian communities.

One of the biggest impacts was simply getting people out of their cars. Walking to work, to the store, to community meeting places, or to nature preserves brings people into direct contact with the other members of the community. People walking together in the same direction naturally converse, establishing friendships, informing each other of current events, and discussing issues of relevance to the community. In fact, developing community and social capital has become one of many explicit goals for designing built capital. Modern communities are very healthy places for humans and other species. Invigorating exercise and nurturing social interaction have replaced the stress of hour-long commutes, road rage, and the pollution of vehicle exhaust, improving both physical and mental health. Air quality is very high. Many roads and parking lots have become redundant, and in their spaces stand parks, streams, and greenways, providing clean air, clean water, and healthy recreation, among numerous other vital ecosystem services. The dramatic reduction in impervious areas has reduced flooding and allowed the land and the ecosystems it sustains to filter water, restoring waterways to health.

With scarcer resources, the practice of destroying still useful buildings to build others on the same site has diminished, and stable populations have further decreased the need for new construction. But from time to time new buildings are still required. Ecologically designed "living buildings" have become the norm for new construction.

Transportation: As already mentioned in the description of communities, single-occupancy vehicles are now rare. The dominant modes of transportation within communities are walking and bicycling; between communities people use high-speed rail. Public transportation is important within communities and is designed to transport goods as well as passengers, making it convenient for grocery shopping and the like. Because so many people use public transportation, it is abundant and extremely convenient. Rail is common, but so are electric buses and taxis. "Traffic" is a thing of the past, and public transportation gets people around much more quickly than private vehicles used to, at a fraction of the cost. Dramatically fewer vehicles on the roads has also cut maintenance costs to a fraction of what they were, and new roads are unnecessary. Some people still own private vehicles, but these vehicles are expensive and their owners pay a higher share of costs of road-maintenance coasts. Most communities have electric cars, such as ZipCars, available for rent when private transportation is absolutely required. When not being driven, these cars provide electric energy storage.

Energy: Renewable resources now meet virtually all of the world's energy needs. The conversion from hydrocarbons was facilitated by continuous increases in efficiency of energy use, combined with appropriate full-cost pricing of all energy sources, including environmental and health costs and risks of the full fuel cycle. Photovoltaic tiles are ubiquitous roofing materials, and roofs alone meet over half the world's energy needs. Large-scale hydropower has decreased in importance as more and more rivers are restored to their natural states, but low-impact mini-turbines are increasingly common. In spite of the abundance of nonrenewable, nonpolluting forms of energy, energy-efficiency research is still very important and advances are still being made in both renewable-energy supply and demand management. The "smart grid" has done much to help this transition. In many places municipalities and/or cooperatives now locally manage the generation, supply, and distribution of renewable energy resources, keeping prices affordable and ownership democratically controlled.

Industry: Industry has changed dramatically. Industrial design is now based on closed-loop systems in imitation of nature, where the waste product from one industry becomes the feedstock of the next. Wasted heat from industrial processes is used to heat nearby homes and workspaces. When possible, industrial production uses local materials to meet local needs, and wastes (the few that are not put to use) are processed locally. Most smaller-scale industries consist of a mix of locally owned proprietary firms and smaller corporations on the one hand, and cooperatives and new community-based commons institutions on the other [33]. While these characteristics do not always maximize productive efficiency, the benefits outweigh the costs.

First, local production dramatically reduces transportation costs, helping to compensate for sometimes-higher production costs. Second, it makes communities directly aware of the environmental impacts of production and consumption. Costs of waste disposal are not shifted elsewhere. Third, industries are more a part of their communities. Most of them are locally owned by the workers they employ, by new cooperative and municipal institutions, and by the people whose needs they meet. Rather than simply trying to maximize returns to shareholders, industries strive to provide healthy, safe, secure, and fulfilling working conditions for workers.

Those who produce goods and those who consume them know each other, so workers take particular pride in the quality of what they produce.

Fourth, the decentralization of the economy means that the economy as a whole is much less susceptible to business cycles, increasing job and community stability—a central requirement of local sustainability planning in general. Fifth, an emphasis on local ownership and production for local markets has reduced the importance of trade secrets and patents; competition has been replaced to some extent by cooperation.

Sixth, a significant number of larger firms are structured as public and quasi-public enterprises jointly owned with the workers involved. They are designed, on the one hand, to help target and anchor jobs to help achieve local stability, thereby also supporting sustainability planning, and on the other, to be less dependent on very short-term profit considerations necessary to meet stock market expectations that foster excessive growth.

Finally, decreased competition has led to a dramatic decrease in the size of the advertising industry. This means that money once spent on convincing people to buy one brand over another is now spent on making those products better—or simply not spent, making those products more affordable.

Markets and competition, of course, still play an important role. Industries are free to sell to distant communities, though having to pay the full cost of transportation provides a natural barrier. Still, this threat of competition means that communities need not rely solely on the good will of local industries to keep prices low. Trade secrets play less of a role in competition than in the past due to the resurgence of sharing information. The development of open-source software shows that freely sharing knowledge can lead to more rapid technological innovation than the profit motive provided by privatizing knowledge through patents. The problems with patents have became more obvious with the tremendous growth in green technologies, which have proven themselves capable of slowing climate change, reducing pollution, and decreasing demands on scarce ecosystem resources, but only by being used on a large scale. Patents on these technologies (and the accompanying monopoly profits) would mean that much of the world would be unable to afford them. The global community has come to realize that it cannot afford the price of people not using these technologies.

Fortunately, the free flow of information has led to impressive new innovations, often making patents obsolete. Some industries retain substantial economies of scale, using fewer resources per unit when producing in enormous factories. This is still the case for solar cells, for example. Large corporations still exist to produce such goods, but many are structured in ways that broaden representation on boards and in certain cases entail public ownership or joint public/worker ownership. Corporate charters have largely changed to the "benefit corporation" model that explicitly acknowledges a firm's responsibility to produce a social benefit rather than merely a private profit.

2.3. Human Capital

Human capital was defined in the early part of the century as the practical knowledge, acquired skills, and learned abilities of an individual that make him or her potentially productive and thus equip him or her to earn income in exchange for labor.

The definition of human capital itself has changed—no longer emphasizing solely productivity in terms of income exchanged for labor. The primary emphasis instead is now on knowledge, skills, and abilities that make people productive members of society. The goals of society are far more than simply earning income. Education is now integrated into everyday life, not simply something we do for a few hours a day before we grow up. And it is not always confined to classrooms—schools are an institution, not a physical place. Nature offers us an amazing laboratory every time we step outside, and is valued every bit as much in urban settings as in rural. This is even more true in 2050, when our communities are designed to maximize exposure to healthy ecosystems. Education about civic responsibilities and roles is heavily stressed, and such topics are taught by direct exposure to the decision-making process or hands-on participation in activities that benefit the community. Youth are schooled in civic responsibility by actively participating in the community. And what better place to learn skills required for economic production than at the workplace? Apprenticeships are now an integral part of the learning process. Technology also plays an important role in education. Online learning environments are used where appropriate but by no means replace direct interaction. Education is now an interactive balance between online tools and content acquisition, and on-the-ground problem solving in the community.

Education and science no longer focus solely on the reductionist approach, in which students are only taught to analyze problems by breaking them down into their component parts. While the reductionist approach and analysis still play an important role in education, the emphasis is now on synthesis—how to rebuild the analyzed components of a problem into a holistic picture to solve problems. Synthesis is critical for understanding system processes, and system processes dominate our lives.

Beyond analysis and synthesis, learning also now emphasizes communication. Researchers skilled at communication are able to more readily share ideas, and ideas grow through sharing. Workers skilled at communication are able to work together to solve production problems. Citizens skilled at communication are able to contribute to the ever-evolving vision of a sustainable and desirable future that is the motivating force behind policy and governance. Citizens are also able to communicate their knowledge with each other, so that education, livelihood, family, and community become a seamless whole of lifelong learning and teaching, everyone simultaneously a student and teacher.

Education also now emphasizes much more than just scientific understanding of the material world. Critical thinking and research are important, but so are creative expression and curiosity. Knowledge and science are not portrayed as value-neutral endeavors; students now learn that the very decision of what to study is a moral choice with broad implications for society. The goal of education is to cultivate wisdom and discernment, to cultivate the emotional maturity to allow responsible decision making in every type of human endeavor.

The whole notion of work has also changed, and the word itself has lost the connotation of an unpleasant chore. Work hours have been reduced through work sharing and more generous leave policies to allow for a more reasonable balance of family and work life. Moreover, people now recognize the absurdity of applying technology to the problem of producing more goods to be consumed during leisure time regardless of the drudgery involved in the production process itself. Instead, to recruit the needed workers, industry is now forced to redirect some of its technological prowess toward making work itself a pleasurable part of our days that engages both mental and physical skills. A typical job now involves far more variety, not only to make work more exciting and interesting, but also to take advantage of the full range of a person's skills. There is less distinction between what would have earlier been considered gainful employment and volunteer work.

Everyone participates in civil society, both in decision making and in maintaining the public space. This is not an onerous chore, but a pleasurable time for socializing with neighbors and community. Nor does it take time away from private lives, since the typical work week in traditional jobs now averages only 15 hours. Education deemphasizes the old "more is better" mindset and promotes a greater understanding of the linkages between economic production, nature, human development, and society. This has made people more aware of the true costs of excessive consumption.

With years of technological advance and diminished "needs," society is now able to provide a satisfactory living wage to all who work and to meet the basic needs of those who do not. Participation in the various types of work is expected and supported, but not forced. Because work is now more a fulfilling experience than an onerous necessity, there is little resentment of those who do not work but rather a feeling of concern that these people are not developing their potential as humans. Living in more tightly knit communities where social goals are actively discussed, people now better understand the importance of their work and feel greater obligation to contribute to the common good. Remuneration for work has been restructured to provide the greatest awards to those who provide the greatest amount of service to the community, such as teachers, childcare providers, and so on.

Human capital is also directly related to human populations. The population has stabilized at a level compatible with the safe operating space of our planet.

2.4. Social Capital

Social capital refers to the institutions, relationships, and norms that shape the quality and quantity of a society's social interactions. Social capital is not just the sum of a society's institutions, which underpin that society; it is the glue that holds them together.

The dominant form of social capital in the employment and economic sphere in the early part of the century was the market. The interaction between employer and employee was that of buying and selling labor. In this model, employer loyalty exists only as long as the continued employment of the employee increases profits. Employee loyalty exists only as long as no other job offers a greater salary or better fringe benefits (which may include location, working conditions, etc.). The interaction between producer and consumer is even more market-based in this model. People buy a product only as long as it is perceived to provide the greatest value in monetary terms, though admittedly advertising may play as large a role in shaping perceptions as the actual price and quality of the product.

In 2050, worker and worker/community ownership of many industries and local production for local markets has changed these relationships. Such enterprises logically pay more attention to worker and community well-being than enterprises driven by the need to generate shareholder profit. Well-being, of course, includes profit-shares but is increased by working conditions that are healthy, that stimulate creativity, and that create feelings of participation, community, and identity. While not all enterprises are owned in these ways, when a significant percentage of enterprises began to offer these conditions, they put pressure on the others to do so as well. In the absence of strong social capital, local production for local markets can be a disaster. In many cases, it might be inefficient to have a number of firms providing similar products for a small community. This could lead to monopoly provision of certain goods. If the market had remained the dominant form of social capital driving interactions between producers and consumers, high profits and poor quality would have resulted. However, when worker-owners also live in the local community, they have to answer to their neighbors for both the price and quality of what they produce. High-quality production is a source of pride, while low quality and high prices are perceived as incompetence and laziness, decreasing the individual's social standing in the community.

Local currencies also now contribute significantly to locally based production and consumption. Such systems existed in many communities in the early part of the century, such as in Ithaca, New York (http://www.ithacahours.org) and the Berkshires in western Massachusetts (http://www.berkshares.org). These currencies are backed only by trust that other members of the community will accept them in exchange for goods and services, and therefore require strong social capital to function. They also build social capital every time a community member accepts the currency. They are virtually immune to national and global economic instability and provide communities with greater autonomy.

For local markets to work, social capital must be strong. As discussed in the section on built capital, the very physical structure of communities now works to create that social capital. Abundant community spaces, parks, and recreation areas stimulate social interaction, build friendships, and generate a sense of responsibility toward neighbors and community. With single-occupancy vehicles almost gone and people living in smaller communities, just getting from place to place brings people in close contact with their neighbors.

At the beginning of the century, public transportation was primarily found only in large cities, and fellow passengers were strangers, not neighbors. Under these circumstances, public transportation did little to build social capital. But this is no longer the case in 2050. Some neighborhoods coalesced around different ethnicities and cultures, and these too served as sources of social capital. However, the world has rid itself of the racism, sexism, regionalism, and other prejudices that were all too prevalent earlier. People have more time for family, and family life is characterized by more balanced gender roles.

The process of government itself now creates social capital. Many countries are no longer weak representative democracies, but strong participatory ones. In a participatory democracy, the people must discuss at length the issues that affect them to decide together how the issues should be resolved. In the old world—of high-pressure jobs, little free time, and large communities of anonymous strangers—this approach to government seemed impractical, unwieldy, and too demanding. Now, with smaller communities of neighbors, a far shorter work week, and engaged, active citizens, participatory democracy is a privilege of citizenship and not an onerous chore. Of course, this required that civic education form an essential part of education and development of human capital from childhood on. This approach to government is particularly effective at the local level. As citizens come together in regular meetings to discuss the issues and work together to resolve them (even when substantial conflict exists), it creates strong bonds of social capital and plays an essential role in forging a sense of community.

Government, of course, implies action, and action implies purpose. The purpose must be defined by the people, who in these civic meetings also forge a shared vision of the future to guide their actions. This vision is not static but must adapt to new information and new conditions as they emerge. Of course, not all issues can be decided on the local level. Institutions are required at the scale of the problems they address. It is at the local level where people will feel the consequences of ecosystem change, for example, but causes may be distant, perhaps in other countries. On the national level it is not feasible to bring together millions of people to discuss the issues and decide on actions, so some form of representation is required. But representatives are now chosen through direct participation by people to whom they have strong social ties and obligations, so these representatives are far more likely to truly represent their communities and not some large corporation that funds their rise to power. Additionally, new intermediary representative institutions on the regional scale exist to bridge the gap between local and national governance.

Social capital, the glue that holds society together, also include basic moral values and ethics such as honesty, fair dealing, care for the disabled, and a common set of cultural practices and expectations that for the majority do not have to be enforced by law. Both markets and government bureaucracies fail without these common values. These values are rooted in community and nurtured by the religions of the world and other systems of thought and practice. Social capital has deep roots, and has been depleted in many areas.

2.5. Natural Capital

Natural capital consists of all the world's ecosystems - their structure and processes that contribute to the well-being of humans and every other species on the planet. This includes both mineral and biological raw materials, renewable (solar, wind and tidal) energy and fossil fuels, waste-assimilation capacity, and vital life-support functions (such as global climate regulation) provided by well-functioning ecosystems.

The absolute essentiality of natural capital is now so completely accepted that it is taken for granted that we must protect it if we are to survive and thrive as a species. Any schoolchild is able to tell you that you cannot make something from nothing, so all economic production must ultimately depend on raw material inputs. Economic production is a process of transformation, and all transformation requires energy inputs. It is equally impossible to make nothing from something, so every time we use raw materials to make something, when that product eventually wears out, it returns to nature as waste. It is therefore incumbent upon us to make sure that those wastes can be processed by the planet's ecosystems. Waste-absorption capacity is only one of many critical but still scarcely understood services provided by intact ecosystems. These ecosystem services include regulation of atmospheric gases, regulation of water cycles and the provision of clean water, stabilization of the global climate, protection from ultraviolet radiation, and the sustenance of global biodiversity, among many others. Without these services, human life itself would be impossible.

While by 2050, we have made substantial efforts to protect ecosystem services, uncontrolled human economic activity still has the capacity to damage them sufficiently to threaten our civilization. Obviously, well-functioning ecosystems are composed of the same plants and animals that serve as raw-material inputs to the economy; and, all else being equal, increasing raw-material inputs means diminished ecosystem services. Extraction of renewable raw materials directly diminishes ecosystem services, while the extraction of mineral resources unavoidably causes collateral damage to ecosystems. Ecosystem services are also threatened by waste outputs. While waste outputs from renewable resources are, in general, fairly readily assimilated and broken down by healthy ecosystems, ecosystems have not evolved a similar capacity to break down waste products from mining and industry, concentrated heavy metals, fossil fuels, and synthesized chemicals. In 2050 we have dramatically decreased our reliance on these slow-to-assimilate materials.

Natural capital is also economically important because it provides so many insights into the production process. The more we have learned about how nature produces, the more we have realized the inefficiency, toxicity, and wastefulness of former production techniques. It has now become a standard approach when seeking to solve a production problem to examine healthy ecosystems and strive to understand how they "solve" similar problems.

A recognition and high level of awareness of the importance of natural capital have led to dramatic changes in the way it is treated. The negative environmental impacts of nonrenewable resource use, even more than such materials' growing scarcity, have forced us to substitute renewable resources for nonrenewables, reversing the trend that began with the Industrial Revolution and making renewables more valuable than ever. Passive investment in natural capital stocks—that is, simply letting systems grow through their own reproductive capacity—is insufficient to meet our needs. Active investment is required. We are actively engaged in restoring and rebuilding our natural capital stocks by planting forests, restoring wetlands, and increasing soil fertility. The former philosophy of natural capital as free goods provided by nature has disappeared. This change has required and inspired significant institutional changes. For example, notions of property rights to natural capital have changed. Most forms of natural capital are now recognized as intergenerational assets. For example, legislation in many countries now explicitly prohibits the extraction of renewable resources beyond the rate at which they can replenish themselves, which would leave future populations dependent for survival on nonrenewable resources in danger of exhaustion and for which no substitutes exist.

Property rights to land are explicitly extended to future generations, and there are steep fines or even criminal penalties for leaving land in worse condition than when it was purchased. While ecological factors determine the total amount of natural capital that we can safely deplete, market forces still determine how that natural capital should be allocated. In addition to these fixed limits on resource use, green taxes now force both consumers and producers to pay for the damage caused by resource depletion and waste emission. When these costs are unknown, those undertaking potentially harmful activities are forced to purchase bonds or insurance that guarantee reimbursement to society for whatever damages do occur. These policies have dramatically increased the costs of degrading natural capital. As a result, most countries are rapidly weaning themselves from dependence on nonrenewable resources, having developed renewable substitutes for most of them. Many countries are competing to become global leaders in green technology. While we once relied on hydrocarbons as a feedstock for many industrial processes, we now rely heavily on carbohydrates produced by plants. This allows us to build nontoxic, biodegradable carbon polymers from CO_2 extracted directly from the atmosphere. As this technology came into its own, it helped to stabilize and even reduce atmospheric CO_2. Whether we will be able to continue to reduce global warming is still an open question, but one with growing cause for optimism.

Our understanding of ecosystem function has progressed dramatically and we continue to discover new ecosystem services. Yet for every puzzle we solve, we uncover three others. And we remain unable to accurately predict impacts of human activities on specific ecosystems, in part because of ongoing changes induced by continued global change. While the rate of warming has slowed, ecosystems are still slowly adapting to the impacts of that warming. The precautionary principle therefore now plays a critical role in deciding how we treat the environment when there is doubt over the potential impact of resource extraction or waste emissions on ecosystem goods and services. We choose to err on the side of caution. Continuing ecological-restoration efforts have begun to reverse the massive degradation that took place from 1950 through 2020, but continued global warming still threatens dangerous disruptions in ecosystem services. In keeping with the precautionary principle, we now consider it an imperative to develop extensive ecological buffers and to take the idea of planetary boundaries seriously.

3. A Redesign of "the Economy" Recognizing Its Embeddedness in Society and Nature

To achieve the vision outlined in the previous section will require some fundamental changes. As Meadows has pointed out, there is a spectrum of ways we can intervene in systems [38]. She lists 12 leverage points (shown on the right) for changing systems, ranging from changing parameters all the way to changing basic worldviews. We believe that the transition to a sustainable and desirable society will require a fundamental redesign of our system utilizing all of the leverage points. But most fundamentally, it will require changing worldviews, as outlined in the vision section above. Below, we outline some of the policy, governance, and institutional design implications of that change in worldview.

Leverage Points for Changing Complex Systems

12. **Numbers:** Constants and parameters such as subsidies, taxes, and standards

11. **Buffers:** The sizes of stabilizing stocks relative to their flows

10. **Stock-and-Flow Structures:** Physical systems and their nodes of intersection

9. **Delays:** The lengths of time relative to the rates of system changes

8. **Balancing Feedback Loops:** The strength of the feedbacks relative to the impacts they are trying to correct

7. **Reinforcing Feedback Loops:** The strength of the gain of driving loops

6. **Information Flows:** The structure of who does and does not have access to information

5. **Rules:** Incentives, punishments, constraints

4. **Self-Organization:** The power to add, change, or evolve system structure

3. **Goals:** The purpose or function of the system

2. **Paradigms:** The mindset out of which the system—its goals, structure, rules, delays, parameters—arises.

1. **Transcending Paradigms**

The problems we face—overconsumption, overpopulation, fossil fuel use, and destruction of species—are not mainly technical problems. If they were, we'd be able to solve them within a few years. The systems involved are complex and interconnected in ways that make their behavior inherently unpredictable. "As a result, the politics of communities' and nations' efforts to address their sustainability problems is much more important than any technical expertise they can muster" [34]. There are experts aplenty, but we cannot simply consult them for the "best" solutions, because nobody can know what those solutions are in any complete or final sense. The solutions must be explored and tested through a process of continuous adaptive learning. Deciding which options to try means making political choices that affect everyone and require wide support and engagement. A generation after its coinage, the slogan "Power to the People" takes on a new meaning.

Because there can be no permanent solutions in a world that is ecologically and culturally dynamic, these choices will have to be made again and again as circumstances evolve. Therefore, moving toward a sustainable and desirable future will require a radically broadened base of participants and a political process that continuously keeps them engaged. The process must encourage the perpetual hearing, testing, working through, and modification of visions at multiple scales, from local to global.

The key seems to be structuring political systems so that people's decisions matter. What does all this mean? It means the most important issue we all face is democratic control of our lives. In a very real sense, all the issues of poverty, environment, justice, and community boil down to failures of democratic participation. When we complain about corporate power and the destructive effects of "globalization," we are complaining about the absence of democratic decision-making (decision-making by those who are affected by the decisions). We all want democracy. But how much time do we devote to studying how to make democracy really work? How much effort do we spend trying to re-arrange our local communities so that we make decisions by talking together? These are good questions. In sum, how can we turn our vision of a sustainable and desirable world into reality? We can start by learning how to make democracy work—really work—in workplaces, in local communities, in cities, in states, in nations, and globally [33]. How can that begin to happen? How can we shift our society from "thin democracy" to "strong democracy" [39,40]?

The key to achieving sustainable governance in the new, full-world context is an integrated (across disciplines, stakeholder groups, and generations) approach based on the paradigm of "adaptive management," whereby policy-making is an iterative experiment acknowledging uncertainty, rather than a static "answer." Within this paradigm, six core principles (the Lisbon principles) that embody the essential criteria for sustainable governance have been identified [41]. The six principles together form an indivisible collection of basic guidelines governing the use of common natural and social capital assets.

- *Principle 1:* Responsibility. Access to common asset resources carries attendant responsibilities to use them in an ecologically sustainable, economically efficient, and socially fair manner. Individual and corporate responsibilities and incentives should be aligned with each other and with broad social and ecological goals.

- *Principle 2:* Scale-matching. Problems of managing natural and social capital assets are rarely confined to a single scale. Decision-making should (1) be assigned to institutional levels that maximize ecological input, (2) ensure the flow of information between institutional levels, (3) take ownership and actors into account, and (4) internalize social costs and benefits. Appropriate scales of governance will be those that have the most relevant information, can respond quickly and efficiently, and are able to integrate across scale boundaries.

- *Principle 3:* Precaution. In the face of uncertainty about potentially irreversible impacts to natural and social capital assets, decisions concerning their use should err on the side of caution. The burden of proof should shift to those whose activities potentially damage natural and social capital.

- *Principle 4:* Adaptive management. Given that some level of uncertainty always exists in common asset management, decision-makers should continuously gather and integrate appropriate ecological, social, and economic information with the goal of adaptive improvement.

- *Principle 5:* Full cost allocation. All of the internal and external costs and benefits, including social and ecological, of alternative decisions concerning the use of natural and social capital should be identified and allocated, to the extent possible. When appropriate, markets should be adjusted to reflect full costs.

- *Principle 6:* Participation. All stakeholders should be engaged in the formulation and implementation of decisions concerning natural and social capital assets. Full stakeholder awareness and participation contributes to credible, accepted rules that identify and assign the corresponding responsibilities appropriately.

Below are examples of worldviews, institutions, and technologies that can help move us toward the new economic paradigm. In this case technologies are broadly defined as the applied information that we use to create human artifacts (printing press) as well as the institutional instruments used to help us meet our goals (taxes) [42]. The list is separated into three primary sections: respecting ecological limits, protecting capabilities for flourishing, and building a sustainable macro-economy. These are further elaborated below.

3.1. Respecting Ecological Limits

Once society has accepted the worldview that the economic system is sustained and contained by our finite global ecosystem, it becomes obvious that we must respect ecological limits. This requires that we understand precisely what these limits entail, and where economic activity currently stands in relation to these limits.

3.1.1. Waste emission stocks and flows

There are several categories of dangerous waste emissions, including nuclear waste, particulates, toxic chemicals, heavy metals, greenhouse gases, and excess nutrients. Here, we focus on just two as examples. One of the most serious problems the planet currently faces is global climate disruption, caused by excessive stocks of greenhouse gases in the atmosphere. Another is the potentially catastrophic effect of excessive nitrogen and phosphorous emissions into aquatic ecosystems. These two categories of waste emissions serve to illustrate the general problem of waste emissions.

Climate change is an example of excessive stocks of waste; flows of the predominant greenhouse gas, carbon dioxide, are harmless if the atmospheric stock is at an acceptable level. Since energy is required to do work, and 86 percent of the energy currently used for economic production comes from fossil fuels, economic activity inevitably generates flows of greenhouse gases into the atmosphere with current technologies. Various ecosystem processes, such as plant growth, soil formation, and dissolution of CO_2 into the ocean, are capable of sequestering CO_2 from the atmosphere. However, if flows into the atmosphere exceed flows out of the atmosphere, then atmospheric stocks will accumulate. This represents a critical ecological threshold for flows, and exceeding it, risks runaway climate change with disastrous consequences. At a minimum then, for any type of waste where accumulated stocks are the main problem, emissions must be reduced below absorption capacity. The Intergovernmental Panel on Climate Change (IPCC) estimates that global ecosystems currently absorb about 20 percent of anthropogenic emissions. Achieving stable atmospheric stocks of CO_2 requires emissions reductions of 80 percent, or else some means to increase the rate at which ecosystems can sequester CO_2.

However, it is also essential to target a sustainable atmospheric stock of CO_2. There is currently considerable debate about what such a stock would be, with two separate levels of uncertainty: first, what level of climate change is tolerable, and second, what level of atmospheric stocks will lead to that level of change. What determines tolerable climate change also has two components. First are the issues of impacts on agriculture, sea level rise, biodiversity loss, and so on. Second is that the threat that warming climate will create positive feedback loops leading to an even warmer climate, causing runaway climate change. There is widespread agreement that 2 degrees C is the maximum acceptable level of change. *The Stern Review on the Economics of Climate Change* argued that we should ideally target 440 parts per million (ppm) CO_2e[1] , which the report estimated would impose a 6-percent chance of exceeding 2 degrees change, but that 550 ppm was a more feasible target even though it would impose a 29-percent risk of exceeding 2 degrees [43]. More recently, Stern has concluded that 440 ppm is the maximum acceptable limit. NASA climatologist James Hansen, in contrast, argues that 350 ppm is the maximum acceptable level, though he is vague about whether this is CO_2 itself or CO_2e [44]. These are all different estimates of the critical ecological thresholds for stocks. Current stocks are in the vicinity of 390 ppm CO_2, and 435 CO_2e.

There is growing evidence that current stocks are indeed already too high. There is clear evidence of global climate change in current weather patterns, and scientists predict that, even if society currently reduced emissions to zero, the climate would continue to warm for another 30 years. Furthermore, the oceans are beginning to acidify as they sequester more CO_2. Acidification threatens the numerous forms of oceanic life that form carbon based shells or skeletons, such as mollusks, corals, and diatoms.

The weight of evidence suggests that we have already exceeded the critical ecological threshold for atmospheric stocks. This means that we must reduce flows by more than 80 percent or increase sequestration until atmospheric stocks are reduced to acceptable levels. At this point flows could be set equal to absorption capacity, with the caveat that it does not lead to excessive acidification of the ocean. If we accept that all individuals are entitled to an equal share of CO_2 absorption capacity, then the wealthy nations would need to reduce net emissions by 95 percent or more. If we believe that wealthy nations should be held accountable for accumulated stocks, they would essentially need to reduce net emissions to zero or less.

Nitrogen and phosphorous emissions are somewhat different. As emission levels increase, they cause excessive growth of plant life, which rapidly sequesters the pollutants. In other words, sequestration rates increase in response to increasing emissions. However, the excessive growth of plant life can seriously disrupt aquatic ecosystems. As the plants die, the bacteria that consume them utilize much of the available oxygen, causing massive dead zones. In this case, the target of emissions reductions is primarily the flow, not the stock.

The rule for limiting waste emissions is that flows cannot be allowed to exceed absorption capacities nor disrupt critical ecological processes. If accumulated stocks already disrupt

---

1 CO_2e is short for CO_2 equivalent. It is measured by converting all greenhouse gases into their CO_2 equivalent in terms of greenhouse effect.

critical ecological processes, then flows must be reduced below absorption capacity until stocks are reduced to acceptable levels. Quantitative restrictions are preferable to price signals, since the latter are ineffective in the presence of growing demand.

3.1.2. Renewable resource stocks, flows, funds, and services

All economic production requires the transformation of raw materials provided by nature. To a large extent, society can choose the rate at which it harvests these raw materials. Whenever extraction rates of renewable resources exceed their regeneration rates, stocks will decline. Extraction typically becomes more expensive as stocks decline, reducing economic benefits. At some point, the regeneration capacity of declining stocks will decline as well. Eventually, the stocks will reach a point at which they are no longer capable of regenerating. The first rule for renewable resource stocks is that extraction rates must not exceed regeneration rates, thus maintaining the stocks to provide appropriate levels of raw materials at an acceptable cost.

However, this simple result ignores the fact that if renewable resources are not used for economic production, they otherwise serve as the structural building blocks of ecosystems. A particular configuration of ecosystem structure generates critical ecosystem services, including both life-support services (without which no species can survive) and the capacity of ecosystems to reproduce themselves. These services are diminished when the structure is depleted or its configuration changed. We cannot simply treat ecosystem structure as a stock that yields a flow of raw materials. We must also treat it as a fund that yields a flux of services over time. The generation of this flux of services does not require the physical transformation of ecosystem structure, and flux occurs at a rate over which we have little control.

The second rule for resource extraction and land use conversion is that they must not threaten the capacity of the ecosystem fund to provide essential services. Furthermore, the marginal economic gains from conversion cannot exceed the marginal ecological costs. In short, we face a macro-allocation problem: determining how much ecosystem structure can be converted to economic production and how much must be conserved in order to supply ecosystem services. If we proceed rationally, the first units of economic production satisfy our most pressing needs. As economic output increases, it goes to satisfy less pressing needs and wants. Furthermore, if we strive to minimize the ecological costs of conversion, we sacrifice the least important components of our ecosystem funds first. As we convert more and more, we most sacrifice increasingly important components, and hence pay increasingly higher ecological costs. When the rising marginal costs of conversion exceed the diminishing marginal benefits, then continued conversion to economic production becomes uneconomic. Our limited understanding of ecosystem structure and function, and the dynamic nature of ecological and economic systems, mean that we cannot pinpoint some precise optimum. However, it is increasingly obvious that economic growth has already become uneconomic. Rates of resource extraction must therefore be reduced to below regeneration rates in order to restore ecosystem funds to desirable levels.

3.1.3. Unacceptable tradeoffs: Ecological and economic thresholds

The necessity for imposing ecological limits on resource extraction and waste emission is straightforward. Failure to respect these limits means ecological catastrophe. However, respecting ecological limits in the short run is likely to impose unacceptable economic costs. Take, for example, the case of CO_2 emissions from fossil fuels. The marginal costs of continued emission rates are unacceptably high. However, our economy is deeply dependent on fossil fuels. Very few of us can own or consume anything that did not require fossil fuels, including food. The economic costs of reducing emissions by over 80 percent in the short run would be unacceptably high.

Food systems are even more important than fossil fuels. Almost 1 billion people are currently malnourished. The global population is expected to increase by another 2 billion by 2050, and rising incomes will likely increase the demand for animal protein, which requires far more land and resources to produce than plant foods. The UN Food and Agriculture Organization therefore estimates that we must increase global food production by 70 percent by 2050, or face malnutrition and even starvation for the world's poor [45]. Clearly, the benefits of agriculture are extremely high. At the same time, of the nine planetary boundaries discussed by Rockström and colleagues, agriculture is the leading threat to five of them (biodiversity loss, nitrogen and phosphorous loading, land use change, and freshwater use) and a major contributor to several others [1]. The last significant source of wild food, oceanic fisheries, is also serious depleted, posing significant threats to marine ecosystem services [46]. Even current levels of food production may have unacceptably high ecological marginal costs, and increasing output by 70 percent certainly would. Goodland and Anhang have determined that the lifecycle and supply-chain impacts of livestock production account for at least half of anthropogenic greenhouse gases in the form of methane [47]. Since methane is a more potent greenhouse gas than CO_2 and has a shorter half-life in the atmosphere, a reduction of flows of methane now will have a larger and quicker effect on global warming than CO_2 reductions. As a result, a 25-percent reduction in meat production would almost fully achieve the goals of the recent (failed) international climate conferences. Replacing livestock products with alternatives can also decrease forest burning and allow for substantial regeneration of forest [47]. So it is the only available strategy for both reducing emissions and increasing carbon capture on a large scale in the timeframe during which it is widely agreed that climate change must be addressed.

3.1.4. Redirecting technology toward sustainable solutions

Conventional economists have long assumed that technological progress would overcome any resource constraints and allow endless economic growth [48]. A far less challenging, but still formidable, goal for technological progress would be to help stave off the looming crises already caused by endless growth described above. To do this, we would need to make rapid progress on alternative energy technologies and develop alternative approaches to agriculture. Given the urgency of the problem, we must assess various types of institutions and disseminate these technologies as quickly as possible.

Today, much research and development is performed by corporations driven by economic incenives. But, there are a number of serious problems inherent to market driven research. First, it can be difficult and expensive to make information excludable (i.e. to prevent people from benefiting from information unless they pay). The private sector is unlikely to produce non-excludable information, since other firms can simply copy it at low cost, giving them a competitive edge over the firm that actually invested in it. Patents can make information relatively excludable, but then anyone who uses that information in subsequent inventions must pay for the right to do so. Unfortunately technologies that generate public goods (such as climate stability) or that meet the needs of the poor (such as affordable food) produce no revenue to pay patent royalties. Such royalties are therefore an added deterrent to generating these technologies. For example, some scientists developed golden rice, a genetically modified strain that produces vitamin A and improves quality of life for the malnourished poor. However, after developing this technology, the scientists discovered that they had potentially infringed on 70 separate patents, which have proved a serious obstacle to distributing the rice to poor farmers [49].

The solution to the conflict between food production and ecosystem services would appear to be agro-ecology - projects that increase the provision of ecosystem services from agricultural land and also increase food production and farmer income from ecological restoration [50]. However, the private sector generally fails to invest in agro-ecology [51], favoring instead technologies that increase market production at the expense of ecosystems.

Alternative energy supplies are also critical. However, the energy sector is among the least innovative of all industries, investing only about 6 percent as much in research and development as the manufacturing sector [52]. Private sector investment in energy technology (research development and employment) has in fact fallen steadily since the 1980s, and accounts for only 0.03 percent of sales revenue in the United States [53].

Cooperative, public-sector investment efforts, in contrast, would address these problems. The public sector by definition is interested in the provision of public goods. Research financed by the public sector can be made freely available for all to use, eliminating the costs of protecting intellectual property rights. A meta-study of returns to research and development typically conducted by the public sector found average annual rates of return of 80 percent [54].

Markets are simply ill-suited for producing information at lowest possible cost. The most important input into new technologies is existing knowledge; information is like grass that grows longer the more it is grazed. When patents raise the price of accessing this knowledge, it raises the price of developing new information.

Furthermore, markets reduce the value of information once it has been developed. If a firm develops a clean, decentralized, inexpensive, and safe alternative to fossil fuels, it would be able to sell the technology at a very high cost, potentially too high for firms in developing countries to afford. These firms would then continue to burn coal and other fossil fuels, leading to continued global climate change. Paradoxically, the value of information is maximized at a price of zero, but at this price there is zero incentive for markets to provide the technology. The solution is not to create private property rights that reduce the value of information, but rather the cooperative, public provision of green technologies that are freely available for all to use.

Since many of the most serious threats to global ecosystems were caused by the excessive consumption of the wealthiest nations, those same nations should provide the bulk of the funding required for R&D in the green technologies that solve those problems. Ideally, all nations would contribute to such an effort to the best of their abilities. Many economists are worried that some nations would free-ride on investments by others. However, free-riding on certain technologies would help protect the environment and also provide benefits to those countries that made the initial investments.

3.1.5. Stabilization of population

One potential solution to these apparently irreconcilable goals is to stabilize or even reduce global populations. With a world population that is surpassing 7 billion, increasing in food and energy prices due to lack of resources [55], slowing of development in already underdeveloped countries due to overpopulation [56,57], and a lack of jobs [58], there has been a refocusing on population stability, often in the form of family-planning policies. Family-planning has been proven to be very cost effective [59]: for every dollar spent on family planning, the United Nations has found that two to six dollars can be saved in the future on other development goals [60]. Recently the United States and the United Kingdom once again increased their foreign aid funding towards international family planning [61].

An estimated one-third of global births is the result of unintended pregnancy [62]. More than 200 million women in developing countries would prefer to delay their next pregnancy or not have any more children at all [63]. However, several barriers prevent many of these women from making a conscious choice: lack of access to contraceptives, risk of side effects, cultural values, or opposition from family members [64,65].

One of the major impacts of such population growth is the negative impact it is having on the earth's life-supporting ecosystem services [66-68]. It has been estimated that about half of the productivity of the earth's biosystems has been diverted to human use [69,70]. As population continues to increase, competition for these increasingly scarce resources will intensify globally. The disconnect between the "haves" and the "have nots" will also become more visible as living standards drop below survival level [71].

However, if we do succeed in stabilizing, or even decreasing, the global population, other problems become apparent. With a non-growing population, the average age of the population increases, creating a situation where more retirees exist relative to workers. Addressing this problem may require higher taxes, extensions of retirement age, and/or pension reductions [72].

3.2. Protecting Capabilities for Flourishing

3.2.1. Sharing the work

In a zero-growth or contracting economy, working-time policies are essential for two main reasons: to achieve macro-economic stability and to protect people's jobs and livelihoods. In addition, reduced working hours can increase flourishing by improving the work/life balance. Specific policies should include: reductions in working hours; greater choice for employees about working time; measures to combat discrimination against part-time work as regards grading, promotion, training, security of employment, rate of pay, health insurance, etc.; and better incentives to employees (and flexibility for employers) for family time, parental leave, and sabbatical breaks [72].[2]

However, achieving hourly reductions will require structural changes in the operation of labor markets. Indeed, even the proximate causes of rising hours are complex. In the United States, factors include the movement of women into full-time career jobs, an upward shift in work norms made possible by the growing power of employers relative to employees, and the collapse of hourly wages at the bottom of the wage distribution (which necessitates longer hours to avoid costly declines in household income) [73]. Higher levels of income inequality have also led workers to prefer longer hours [74,75].

---

2 Much of this section was taken from reference 72. Jackson T (2009) Prosperity without growth: Economics for a finite planet: Earthscan/James & James.

Workers' preferences for income and consumer goods affect the determination of hours but are mainly endogenous, i.e., they adjust to the level of hours, income, and consumption that the market delivers, rather than exogenous preferences that drive the market. The phenomenon of preference endogeneity, preferences that adapt to market outcomes, rather than being fixed, may be more important than has heretofore been recognized [73]. This endogenous preference view is the reverse of the conventional wisdom, which is that workers' exogenous preferences determine the level of hours. It is also quite different from historical accounts that emphasize consumer desires and unionizing strategy as the leading variable in determining hours, and hence the level of output and growth [76].

To date, no detailed empirical studies linking environmental degradation and hours of work exist. Yet, in the simplest models, in which hours are correlated with income and hence consumption, a reduction in hours *ceteris paribus* (other factors being held equal) would reduce impact [73]. The increased presence of Western media and advertising, the expansion of transnational corporations into domestic markets in the global South, and the development in the South of large middle classes with disposable income are part of a process of rapid growth in branded consumer goods worldwide. In addition to cultural products these include apparel, vehicles, consumer electronics, fast food, travel and tourism, and a range of household durables. In general, this shift is associated with much higher levels of environmental impact [77].

However, many of the productivity gains of the past 200 years were driven by a shift from human labor to fossil fuels. There is therefore a distinct possibility that a dramatic reduction in fossil fuel use will lead to a shift from capital to labor. It takes approximately 5,000 hours of human labor to generate the work in a barrel of oil [78]. At US$100 a barrel, labor can only compete with oil at $0.02/hour.

3.2.2. Tackling systemic inequality

Social inequality can express itself in many forms besides income inequality, such as life expectancy, poverty, malnourishment, and infant morality [79]. Inequality can be seen between countries but also within countries and small communities. Inequality can drive other social problems (such as over-consumption), increase anxiety, undermine social capital, and expose lower income households to higher morbidity and lower life satisfaction [72].

In the United States civil service, military, and universities, income inequality ranges within a factor of 15 or 20. Corporate America has a range of 500 or more. Many industrial nations are below 25 [80]. One solution to such inequity is to have people who have reached their weekly or monthly working wage limit either work for nothing at the margin, if they enjoy their work, or devote their extra time to hobbies, public service, or their family. The demand left unmet by those at the top will be filled by those who are below the maximum.

A sense of community, necessary for democracy, is hard to maintain across the vast income differences found in the United States. The main justification for such differences has been that they stimulate growth, which will one day filter down, making everyone rich. This may have had plausibility in an empty world, but in our full world, it is unrealistic.

Without aggregate growth, poverty reduction requires redistribution. Complete equality is unfair; unlimited inequality is unfair. Fair limits to the range of inequality need to be determined, i.e., a minimum income and a maximum income [80]. Studies have also shown that the majority of adults would be willing to give up personal gain in return for reducing inequality they see as unfair [81,82].

Other redistributive mechanisms and policies have also been well-established and could include revised income tax structures as discussed above, improved access to high-quality education, anti-discrimination legislation, implementing anti-crime measures and improving the local environment in deprived areas, and addressing the impact of immigration on urban and rural poverty [72]. New forms of cooperative ownership (as in the Mondragón model), or of public ownership, as is common in many European nations, can also help constrain internal pay ratios.

3.2.3. Strengthening human and social capital

Satisfaction of basic human needs requires a balance between social, built, human, and natural capital (and time). Policy and culture help to allocate the four types of capital defined earlier as a means for providing these opportunities.

One institution that helps build social capital is a strong democracy. A strong democracy is most easily understood at the level of community governance, where all citizens are free (and expected) to participate in all political decisions affecting the community. Interactive discussion plays an important role. Broad participation requires the removal of distorting influences like special interest lobbying and funding of political campaigns [83]. In fact, the process itself helps to satisfy myriad human needs, such as enhancing the citizenry's understanding of relevant issues, affirming their sense of belonging and commitment to the community, offering opportunity for expression and cooperation, strengthening the sense of rights and responsibilities, and so on. Historical examples include the town meetings of New England or the system of the ancient Athenians (with the exception that all citizens must be represented, not simply the elite) [34,83].

Participating in society demands that attention be paid to the underlying human and social resources required for this task. Creating resilient social communities is particularly important in the face of economic shocks. Specific policies are needed to create and protect shared public spaces; strengthen community-based sustainability initiatives; reduce geographical labor mobility; provide training for jobs in sustainability; offer better access to lifelong learning and skills; place more responsibility for planning in the hands of local communities; and protect public service broadcasting, museum funding, public libraries, parks and green spaces [72].

3.2.4. Expanding the "commons sector"

Most resource allocation done today is through markets, which are based on private property rights. Private property rights are established when resources can be made "excludable," i.e., one person or group can use a resource while denying access to others. However, many resources essential to human welfare are "non-excludable," meaning that they are difficult or impossible to exclude others from benefiting from these resources. Examples include oceanic fisheries (particularly those beyond the economic exclusion zone), timber from unprotected forests, and numerous ecosystem services, including the waste absorption capacity for unregulated pollutants.

In the absence of property rights, open access to resources exists—anyone who wants to may use them, whether or not they pay. However, individual property rights owners are likely to overexploit or under-provide the resource, imposing costs on others, which is unsustainable, unjust, and inefficient. Private property rights also favor the conversion of ecosystem structure into market products regardless of the difference in contributions that ecosystems and market products have on human welfare. Hence, the incentives are to privatize benefits and socialize costs.

All *scarce* resources are *rival*, meaning that use by one person leaves less of the resource (in quality or quantity) for others to use. Many resources, however, are non-rival, which means that use by one person does not leave less for others to use. When this is true there is no competition for use and the resource is not scarce in an economic sense, even if total supply is inadequate. Examples include streetlights, many different ecosystem services (e.g., climate stability, flood regulation, scenic beauty), and information. Price rationing in this case reduces use and hence value to society without affecting quantity, which is inefficient. For example, if someone develops a cheap, clean solar energy technology and then patents it (which makes it excludable), it can be sold at a price. A positive price will reduce use, leading to less substitution away from competing energy sources, such as coal, and society as a whole suffers. Markets will only provide non-rival resources if they are made excludable and can be sold at a price, but this creates artificial scarcity. Paradoxically, the value of non-rival resources to society is maximized at a price of zero, but at that price markets will not provide it [84].

The solution to these problems lies with common or public ownership. Public ownership can be problematic due to the influence of money in government, which frequently results in the government rewarding the private sector with property rights to natural and social assets. An alternative is to create a commons sector, separate from the public or private sector, with common property rights to resources created by nature or society as whole, and a legally binding mandate to manage them for the equal benefit of all citizens, present and future. The misleadingly labeled "tragedy of the commons" [85] results from no ownership or open access to resources, not common ownership. Abundant research shows that resources owned in common can be effectively managed through collective institutions that assure cooperative compliance with established rules [86-88].

Resources that are rival but non-excludable would need to be "propertized" (made excludable) to prevent over-use [89]. Governments—or in the case of global resources such as atmospheric waste absorption capacity or oceanic fisheries, a global coalition of governments—are generally required to create and enforce property rights, but could turn these rights over to the commons sector as a common assets trust (CAT) [89]. The trust would cap resource use at rates less than or equal to renewal rates, which is compatible with inalienable property rights for future generations. Since the resources under discussion were created by nature, and enforcement of property rights requires the cooperative efforts of society as a whole, rights to the resource should also belong to society as a whole. Individuals who wish to use the resource for private gain must compensate society for the right to do so. This could be achieved through a cap-and-auction scheme, in which the revenue is shared equally among all members of society, or else invested for the common good [90]. Preventing the re-sale of the temporary use-rights would reduce the potential for speculation and private capture of rent. Under common ownership, both costs and benefits accrue to society as whole, and the two are likely to be brought into balance. Taxes on waste emissions and resource extraction can serve the same purpose as a cap-and-auction system.

When a resource is non-rival, excludable property rights are inappropriate, but lack of property rights eliminates private sector incentives to provide the resource. The solution is common investment and common use. The commons sector must invest in the provision of non-rival ecosystem services and in green technologies that help provide and protect such services. Everyone would be free to use the non-rival ecosystem services, but not to degrade the ecosystem structure that sustains them. for the means to invest in non-rival resources can be obtained from auctioning off access to rival resources. For example, the CAT could auction off the right to greenhouse gas absorption capacity, then invest the revenue in carbon-free energy technologies.

When a resource is privately owned but generates economic rent, or is used in a manner that socializes costs and privatizes benefits, taxation can achieve the same goals as common ownership, as discussed in section 4. Table 2 summarizes appropriate property rights for different categories of resources.

Table 2. Rivalry, excludability, and suitable institutions for allocation [84-90].

	Excludable (*rationing is possible*)	**Non-excludable** (*rationing is not possible*)
Rival and scarce (rationing is desirable)	*Potential market resources:* Price rationing may be appropriate, rent should be captured for commons sector by taxes or royalties. Examples: land, timber, oil, absorption capacity for regulated wastes, use of airwaves	*Open access resources:* "Propertization" via collective action is required. Private use rights can be auctioned off by commons sector. Examples: many aquifers, oceanic fisheries, absorption capacity for unregulated wastes
Rival and abundant (rationing is not desirable, except to prevent scarcity)	*Club or toll good:* Price rationing may be appropriate to prevent scarcity; rent should be captured by commons sector. Examples: toll roads, golf courses, ski resorts, private beaches, parks with entrance fees, etc.	*Public good:* Economic growth and ecological degradation are likely to increase scarcity over time. Common sector management is appropriate to prevent scarcity. Examples: oxygen, public beaches
Non-rival (rationing is not desirable; value maximized at a price of zero)	*Inefficient market good:* Price rationing causes artificial scarcity. Common sector provision and ownership would be more efficient. Example: patented information	*Public good:* Commons sector must ensure adequate provision by preventing degradation or investing in provision. Examples: open source information, many ecosystem services

If the public sector shirks its duties to manage our shared social and natural inheritance for the common good, we require a commons sector to ensure sustainability and a just distribution of resources. Once these two goals have been achieved, the market will be far more effective in its role of allocating scarce resources towards the products of highest value, then allocating those products towards the individuals that value them the most.

3.2.5. Removing communication barriers and improving democracy

With the invention of television, political advertisements became a critical outlet for candidates to broadcast their message and to sway voters. However, the decentralized nature of the Internet "allows citizens to gain knowledge about what is done in their name, just as politicians can find out more about those they claim to represent" [91]. As a means of two-way communication, the Internet provides voters the ability to speak out about their government's behavior without leaving their homes. For the Internet to transform the idea of electronic democracy, universal access is critical, but technological, financial, and social barriers currently prevent such universal accessibility [91]. Removal of these and other barriers to engagement and deliberation thus becomes a major goal for replacement of the current plutocracy with real democracy.

Unlike television, very low technological and financial barriers exist to establishing a presence on the Internet. This has the effect of decentralizing information production, and returns control of the distribution of information to the audience, providing a venue for dialogue instead of monologue [92]. Opinions and services previously controlled by small groups or corporations are now shaped by the entire population. Television news networks, sitcoms, and Hollywood productions are being replaced by e-mail, Wikipedia, YouTube, and millions of blogs and forums, all created by the same billions of people who are the audience for the content.

In 2008, the United States presidential election marked the first election year in which more than half of the nation's adult population became involved in the political process by using the Internet as a source of news and information. Rather than simply receiving uni-directional news, approximately one-fifth of the people using the Internet used websites, blogs, social networking sites, and other forums to discuss, comment, and question issues related to the election [93].

3.3. Building a Sustainable Macro-Economy

The central focus of macroeconomic policies is typically to maximize economic growth. This is evident in the definition of a recession as two consecutive quarters with no economic growth. Lesser goals include price stabilization and ensuring full employment. Meadows argues that changing goals is the second most powerful lever for changing complex systems [38]. If society instead adopts the central economic goal of sustainable human well-being, macroeconomic policy will change radically. The goal will be to create an economy that offers meaningful employment to all, that balances investments across the four types of capital to maximize well-being. Recession would be redefined as unacceptable or increasing rates of poverty, misery, inequality, and unemployment, or unsustainable levels of throughput. Such goals would lead to fundamentally different macroeconomic policies and rules. Changing the rules is the third most effective of Meadow's places to intervene in a system.

3.3.1. Changing the institutions: Monetary reform for sustainability and justice

The current monetary system is inherently unsustainable. The base of the money supply in almost all countries is coins and bills printed by governments, and money that governments create when they provide credit to banks during purchases. Government money spent into existence is then destroyed by taxes. Taxes in fact are what give the government the power to create money: everyone accepts government currency because they require it to pay taxes. In the modern era, national currencies are backed by the taxation power of the government. However, this government money (also known as vertical money) is now only a small fraction of the money supply in most economies.

Most of our money supply is now a result of fractional reserve banking. Banks are required by law to retain a percentage of every deposit they receive; the rest they loan at interest. However, loans are then deposited in other banks, which in turn can lend out all but the reserve requirement. The net result is that the new money issued by banks, plus the initial deposit, will be equal to the initial deposit divided by the fractional reserve. For example, if a government credits $1 million to a bank and the fractional reserve requirement is 10 percent, banks can create $9 million in new money, for a total money supply of $10 million. Fractional reserve requirements may not even limit the amount of money created. Banks will typically loan money to any investor who they believe offers a high probability of repayment. If the amount they lend exceeds their reserves, they can borrow money from other banks or the Federal Reserve Bank to make up the deficit. If there is too much borrowing of this type, it threatens to drive up the interest rate. If the Federal Reserve Bank is trying to target interest rates, it will be forced to buy securities from banks to increase bank reserves and the money supply. Regardless of whether the fractional reserve or investor demand determines total money supply, most money is today created as interest-bearing debt. Total debt in the United States, adding together consumers, businesses, and the government, is about $50 trillion dollars. This is the source of the national money supply.

When the loans are repaid, the new money is destroyed. However, the borrowers must repay the loans plus interest and the banks initially loaned out enough to repay only the principal. Either new government expenditures or new loans are required to pay back the interest.

There are several serious problems with this system. First, it is highly destabilizing. When the economy is booming, banks will be eager to loan money and investors will be eager to borrow, which leads to a rapid increase in money supply. This stimulates further growth, encouraging more lending and borrowing, in a positive feedback loop. A booming economy will stimulate firms and households to take on more debt relative to the income flows they use to repay the loans. This means that any slowdown in the economy will make it very difficult for borrowers to meet their debt obligations. Borrowers can sell assets to meet their obligations, but this will drive down the price of assets, for example, home values. Eventually some borrowers will be forced to default. Banks are likely to lose the confidence of other borrowers and will be unwilling to make new loans, which the borrowers require to pay back interest, leading to more defaults. Repayment of loans will exceed creation of loans, leading to a shrinking money supply. Outstanding loans will continue to grow exponentially, even as output diminishes as a result of less money available for investment. Widespread default on the debt becomes inevitable. The result is a self-reinforcing downward economic spiral, leading to recession or worse. The poor usually bear the brunt of the resulting suffering.

Second, the current system systematically transfers resources to the financial sector. Borrowers must always pay back more than they borrowed. At 5.5 percent interest, homeowners will be forced to pay back twice what they borrowed on a 30-year mortgage. Conservatively speaking, interest on the $50 trillion total debt of the United States must be at least $2.5 trillion a year, one-sixth of our national output. Currently, banks can borrow money from the Federal Reserve Bank at almost zero percent, then charge 20 percent or more on credit card debt.

Third, the banking system will only create money to finance market activities that can generate the revenue required to repay the debt plus interest. Since the banking system currently creates far more money than the government, this system prioritizes investments in market goods over public goods, regardless of the relative rates of return to human well-being. Studies find that government investments in public goods regularly generate 25–60 percent non-diminishing annual rates of return, in monetary measures [94]. There is no reason to believe that returns would be any less when the investments are targeted towards the new macroeconomic goals.

Fourth, and most important, the system is ecologically unsustainable. Debt is a lien on future production. Debt grows exponentially, obeying the abstract laws of mathematics. Future production, in contrast, confronts ecological limits and cannot possibly keep pace. Interest rates exceed economic growth rates even in good times. Eventually, the exponentially increasing debt must exceed the value of current real wealth and potential future wealth, and the system collapses. However, in the effort to stave off an economic crisis and the unacceptable misery, poverty, and unemployment it will cause, policy makers will pursue endless economic growth, unsustainable on a finite planet. The system forces us to choose between unsustainable growth and misery.

In order to address this problem, the public sector must reclaim the power to create money, a constitutional right in the United States and most other countries, and take away from the banks the right to do so by gradually moving towards 100-percent fractional reserve requirements. This would allow banks only to loan money on time deposits, in which case the owner of the money forgoes the right to use it while it is loaned to someone else. Banks would be restricted to the role that most people believe they play anyway— serving as an intermediary between those who want to save their money and those who want to borrow it. The current recession is an ideal time to implement this change, since banks are currently loaning far less than allowed by fractional reserves. Reserve deposits in the United States are currently about $1.4 trillion greater than required by law.

The public sector could create money in several different ways. First, the government could simply spend money into existence to provide the public goods that the private sector will not supply, to invest in social and human capital, to create jobs, to rebuild the national infrastructure, and to restore the natural systems that sustain us all. Such spending would end the recession (as previously defined) without increasing the national debt and without systematically transferring interest to the already wealthy. Second, the government could loan money into existence interest-free. Money could be loaned directly to the private sector to finance critical economic activities, such as food production and alternative energy, or it could be loaned to state and local governments (SLGs) to meet their needs. SLGs would also have the option of loaning money interest free or spending it on public goods.

Third, in order to minimize disruption as we change from the current system, the government could make time deposits in banks that serve the common good, allowing them to carry on with business as usual. The public, however, would have control over the money supply.

Ironically, many economists argue that the public sector cannot be trusted to print and spend money—that it will create too much and spend it irresponsibly. The United States government, however, printed $1.6 trillion in government bonds in a single year to finance its deficit, which must be paid back with interest. Issuing interest-free currency is much less risky; it would be difficult for the government to under-perform the private sector when measured by the new goals for macroeconomic policy. At the very least, voters have some control over governments, and none over the banking sector.

There is, however, no free lunch. The government cannot and should not endlessly spend money into existence. The goal must be to achieve a steady state with sustainable levels of throughput, which will likely require a significant reduction in market activity in the wealthy nations, and thus a reduction in the total money supply required to support the economy. When money is loaned into existence, it will be destroyed when it is repaid. State and municipal governments would need to use tax revenue to repay the federal government, but would not need to pay fees to investment banks to issue municipal bonds, nor interest to bond holders. When money is spent into existence, it can be destroyed through taxes, which would play a critical role in regulating the money supply. To ensure that too much money does not flood the economy, any new expenditure could be matched by future taxes, imposed at the same time the expenditure takes place. Rather than a tax, borrow, and spend policy, the government would explicitly pursue a policy of spend, then tax (which, many argue, is actually the way the system currently works anyway). There will no doubt be errors as we shift towards a steady state economy, resulting in occasional recessions or booms. The government however could spend extra money into existence to alleviate misery, poverty, and unemployment during times of recession, and raise taxes if throughput becomes excessive. The monetary system would be counter-cyclical, not pro-cyclical. Government would never need to borrow money and pay it back with interest. There would be no debt. With no exponentially growing debt and no interest payments, there would be no pressure to choose between unacceptable misery or endless growth. The feedback signal of a rising price index would government when to stop creating money.

Fiscal reform is also required to meet the goals of macroeconomic policy. This section is limited to a discussion of taxes, which are a powerful tool for changing economic behavior. The other half of fiscal policy is expenditure, which would be subsumed under monetary policy as described above.

Conventional economists generally look at taxes as a drag on the economy, albeit necessary to finance government expenditures. The reasoning is that taxes increase costs, leading to a reduction in output, and disequilibrium between marginal costs and marginal benefits, resulting in a deadweight loss of economic surplus. They are seen as a significant drag on economic growth. From a more holistic perspective, however, taxes are an effective tool for internalizing negative externalities into market prices, therefore reducing deadweight loss, and for improving income distribution.

3.3.2. Tax bads, not goods

A perennial conflict in tax policy is taxing to raise revenue versus taxing to change behavior. Induced behavioral change aims at avoiding the tax, and this naturally reduces revenue. The policy of shifting the tax base from value added to throughput (that to which value is added) encounters this conflict in a different way. Taxing value added (labor and capital) tends to reduce incentives to enterprise and work, and to use untaxed resources lavishly. Taxing the resource flow would lead to emphasizing resource efficiency, and using less resources (more untaxed recycled resources and more labor and capital) to the extent possible, which is a desired behavioral change, but would reduce revenue. Yet depletion and pollution remain "bads" even if reduced, so there is a good case for further raising the tax on them if revenue needs require it, while value added remains something we want to increase, so we would still want to avoid taxing it.

A shift in the burden of taxation from value added (economic goods, such as income earned by labor and capital) to throughput flow (ecological bads, such as resource extraction and pollution), is critical in shifting towards sustainability [80]. Such a reform would internalize external costs, thus increasing efficiency [95]. It is possible to impose throughput taxes on resource depletion or on waste emissions. Taxing the origin and narrowest point in the throughput flow induces more efficient resource use in production as well as consumption, and facilitates monitoring and collection. For example, there are far fewer oil wells than there are sources of CO_2 emissions. In either case, taxes will increase prices and induce efficiency in resource use. One disadvantage of green taxes is that the level of pollution is determined by price, rather than the ecosystem's capacity to absorb waste. Prices can adjust to ecological constraints more rapidly than ecosystems can respond to the price signals [96]. We discuss below quantitative limits as an alternative.

Many people call for a gradual revenue-neutral tax shift, rather than a set of new taxes. This approach would begin by forgoing a certain dollar amount of revenue from the most regressive taxes, for example, payroll or sales taxes, which currently take a larger percentage of income from the poor than from the rich, while simultaneously collecting the same amount from the best resource severance tax. Then, as the next step, get rid of the second worst tax and substitute the second best resource tax, and so on. As discussed below, however, increasing tax revenue may be desirable.

The logic of ecological tax reform has been broadly accepted for at least a decade and has been implemented in varying degrees across Europe. But progress towards this goal has been painfully slow. In the United Kingdom, the proportion of taxation from green taxes is now lower than it was in 1997. There's an urgent need to achieve an order of magnitude step-change in the structure of taxation. A sustained effort by government is now required to design appropriate mechanisms for shifting the burden of taxation from incomes onto resources and emissions [72].

3.3.3. Tax what we take, not what we make

Taxes should also be used to capture unearned income, or rent, in economic parlance. Green taxes are a form of rent capture, since they charge for the private use of resources created by nature. However, there are many other sources of unearned income in society.

Most obviously, the word "rent" is associated with land. Land is available in a fixed supply which cannot respond to market signals, and is an essential input into all economic activities—even the least tangible economic activities must take place on some physical substrate. The value of land is created by nature and society as a whole, not by individual effort. For example, if a government builds a light rail or subway system—more sustainable alternatives to private cars—adjacent land values typically skyrocket, providing a windfall profit for landowners. New technologies also increase the value of land, due to its role as an essential input into all production [97]. Because the supply of land is fixed, any increase in demand results in an increase in price. Landowners therefore automatically grow wealthier independent from any investments in the land. Furthermore, speculative demand creates a positive feedback loop, in which rising prices increase demand, leading to bubbles and busts in land markets, which can trigger national and even global recessions. High taxes on land values (but not on improvements to land, such as buildings) allow the public sector to capture this unearned income. Similarly, public ownership through land trusts and other means, as is increasingly common, allows for public capture of the unearned income. This removes any reward from land speculation, thus stabilizing the economy. It also drives down land prices. Mortgage payments will be replaced by tax payments, so there will be no negative impact on new landowners. If land values fall, so do payments, dramatically decreasing the likelihood of default and foreclosure. Fixed stocks of land means that it exhibits perfectly inelastic supply, so landowners cannot pass tax increases on to renters.

Growing demand and increasing scarcity of natural resources also drive up their price, generating windfall profits for resource owners. The depletion taxes discussed above should increase in tandem with price increases, capturing the rent for the public sector.

3.3.4. Taxation to reduce inequality

Income inequality can have very pernicious effects on human well-being. Figure 6 below shows the relationship between inequality and an index of health and social problems across OECD countries.

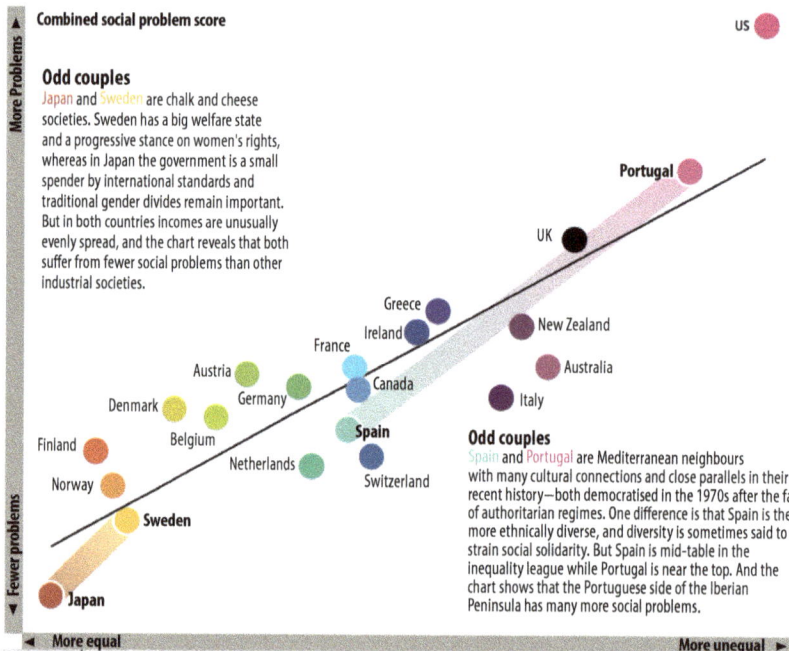

Figure 6. Relationship between income inequality and social problems score in OECD countries [32].

Inequality is also closely related to taxation policies. Figure 7 shows the highest marginal income tax bracket in the United States, along with the share of income captured by the wealthiest 0.1 percent. However, taxes on capital gains, which account for a significant share of the income of the top 0.1 percent, are not included in this figure. The top capital gains tax dropped from 28 percent to 20 percent in 1997, which accounts for the dramatic increase in income inequality beginning that year.

There is also a strong correlation between tax rates and social justice, as evident from Figure 8. High tax rates that contribute to income equality appear to be closely related to human well-being. This suggests that tax rates should be highly progressive, perhaps asymptotically approaching 100 percent on marginal income. The measure of tax justice should not be how much is taxed away, but rather how much income remains after taxes. For example, hedge fund manager John Paulson earned $4.9 billion in 2010 [98]. If Paulson had to pay a flat tax of 99 percent, he would still retain nearly $1 million per week in income. Presumably, most of this income was taxed at the current capital gains tax rate of 15 percent, which also applies to a large share of hedge fund manager income.

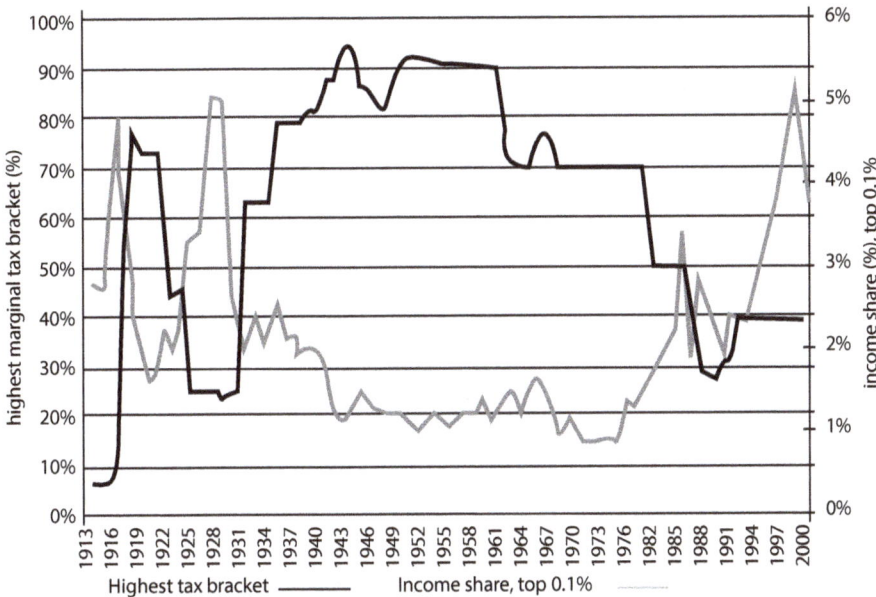

Figure 7. Time series of income in the highest tax bracket in the U.S. (black) and income share in the top 0.1% of households (grey) from 1913 to 2002 [9].

Increasing his tax rate to 99 percent (which might entail a marginal tax rate of 99.99 percent, depending on the tax schedule) would allow the government to hire 84,000 teachers at $49,000 per year.

3.3.5. Increasing financial and fiscal prudence

The monetary reform proposed above requires significant political will, which may be slow in coming. Other policies for achieving financial and fiscal prudence may be required in the meantime.

For over the past decade, debt-driven consumption has pushed economic growth globally. However, our relentless pursuit of that growth as the end goal has contributed to the global economic crisis. A new era of financial and fiscal prudence needs to: increase the regulation of national and international financial markets; incentivize domestic savings, for example through secure (green) national or community-based bonds; outlaw unscrupulous and destabilizing market practices (such as short selling); and provide greater protection against consumer debt [72]. Governments must pass laws that restrict the size of financial sector institutions, eliminating any that impose systemic risks for the economy. "Too big to fail" is "too big to exist."

Certain governmental policies have promoted the financial turmoil of the past few years. Reforming these policies would reduce the distortions within the financial markets, eliminate the too-big-to-fail problem, and prevent the government from manipulating housing credit. These reforms would include: (1) smarter micro-prudential regulation of banks, (2) macro-prudential regulation of bank capital and liquidity standards, (3) creation of credible plans for reforming large, complex banks, (4) elimination of leverage subsidies as a means of promoting homeownership, (5) removal of barriers to stockholder discipline of bank management, (6) policies that promote improvement in counter-party risk management [100], and (7) encouraging sustainable local development through new and existing community, municipal, and state development banking institutions.

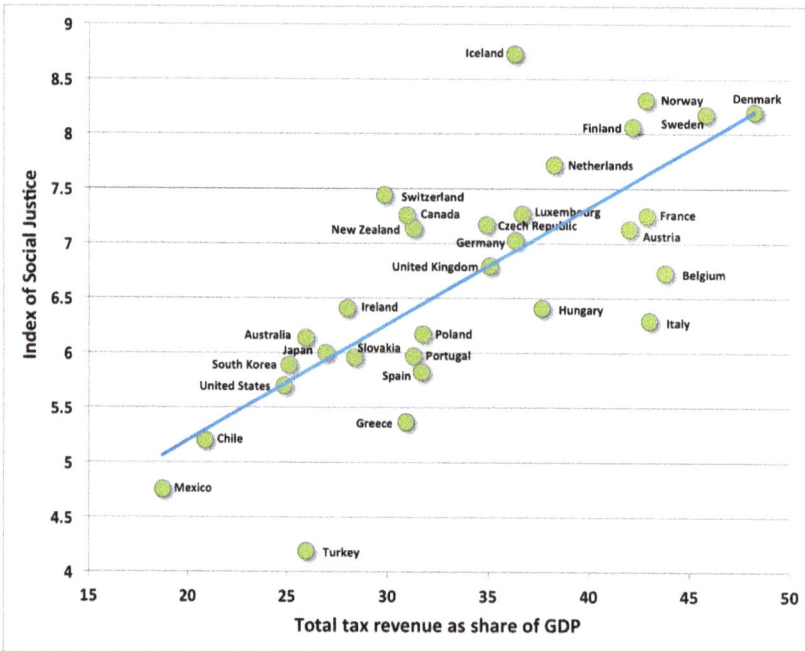

Figure 8. Relationship between tax revenue as a percent of GDP and index of social justice in OECD countries [99].

3.3.6. Improving macro-economic accounting

Unlimited economic growth is not only impossible, it is undesirable. GDP measures costs, not benefits, as illustrated by recent declines in energy and food supply, increasing both their prices and share in GDP even as the benefits they generate decline. An indicator of welfare should measure years of satisfying life, encompassing both quality and quantity.

A large body of literature exists critiquing the value of GDP as a wellbeing measure [101]. Its primary limitations include the following:

1. Failure to account for externalities, both positive (household labor, volunteering, ecosystem services) and negative (pollution, crime, or cancer) [28].

2. Counting the depletion of natural capital as income.

3. Ignoring thresholds beyond which increasing GDP no longer contributes to quality of life. As GDP increases, overall quality of life often increases up to a point. Beyond this point, increases in GDP are offset by the costs associated with increasing income inequality, loss of leisure time, and natural capital depletion [30,102].

4. Failure to account for inequality.

5. Failure to account properly for changes in the asset base, which affect our future consumption possibilities [72].

6. Concentration on flows, when capital stocks may be a better measure of quality of life. Society should seek to minimize the flows required to sustain these stocks [103].

GDP does, however, belong as an indicator of economic efficiency. The more efficient we are, the less economic activity, raw materials, energy, and work it requires to provide satisfying lives. Real efficiency reduces environmental impacts and increases leisure time. As a major cost of providing satisfying lives, GDP does frequently move in parallel with welfare. In the same way, countries that spend more on medical care tend to have better indicators of health. However, concluding that we should therefore maximize medical expenditures, a cost, is absurd. When GDP rises faster than life satisfaction, efficiency declines. Our goal should be to minimize GDP, subject to maintaining a high and sustainable quality of life. The real problem with recession is not that it decreases GDP but that it undermines quality of life by increasing unemployment, poverty, and suffering [42].

In 1969, the United States came to the end of a four-decade decline in income inequality and poverty. People then consumed about half as much per capita as they do today. The genuine progress indicator (GPI), a measure of welfare designed to adjust for the inadequacies of GDP, reached a plateau around this time, and has since declined [30]. Subjective measures of well-being, such as the percentage of people who consider themselves "very happy," have steadily declined since then as well [15]. Empirical evidence therefore suggests that a return to 1969 per-capita consumption levels would not make us worse off. On the contrary, returning to 1969 consumption levels would presumably lower our resource depletion, energy use, and ecological impacts by half, so there is every reason to believe that dramatically lowering our per-capita consumption could actually make us better off [104].

A number of ways of measuring national-level progress has been proposed, developed, and used to address this growing realization that GDP is a measure of economic quantity, not economic quality or welfare, let alone social or environmental well-being.

The measures also address the concern that GDP's emphasis on quantity encourages depletion of social and natural capital and other policies that undermine quality of life for future generations.

In general, these new measures can be categorized as (1) indexes that address the issues described above by making "corrections" to existing GDP accounts, (2) indexes that measure aspects of well-being directly, (3) composite indexes that combine approaches, and (4) indicator suites. Like GDP, all these measures are abstracted indicators, not comprehensive reports on the heart and soul of individual communities. However, some can and are being used to inform local and regional decisions. This is an improvement on the misuse of GDP and economic growth as a proxy for well-being [28].

National accounts should focus on well-being and societal progress as we defined above. Such accounts will provide policy-makers a better chance to react appropriately to financial crises, climate change, and oil price shocks [105]. By utilizing national accounts focused on well-being, a well-being screen will be applied to every policy proposal, allowing a shift away from narrow, income-driven costs/benefits analysis to a wider range of potential impacts on personal and social well-being [106].

3.3.7. Improving macro-economic and regional coordination

Unless planned with care, moving towards a reduced-growth and reduced-time economy could cause many disruptions at the level of firms, communities, and individuals. Current coordination and planning strategies are limited in general, and are focused largely on growth in particular. A new infrastructure capable of generating specific sectoral, geographic, and time allocating alternatives will be required so that choices between alternative paths can become policies rather than scenarios. Developing ways in which larger-order coordination and planning choices can be presented to publics for democratic consideration and decision-making is an essential requirement of the new direction proposed [107].

4. Example Policy Reforms

4.1. Reversing Consumerism

Economic policy has focused almost entirely on promoting continuous growth in GDP. Economic growth often translates into more, instead of better consumption, excessive material and fossil fuel use, and increased waste. The culture of consumerism has developed, in part at least, as a means of enhancing consumption-driven economic growth. But it has had damaging psychological and social impacts on people's well-being. There is a need to systematically dismantle incentives for excessive material consumption and unproductive status competition [11,16].

Excess consumption is driven in part by artificially low prices that fail to reflect full social and environmental costs. Natural resource prices fail to reflect demand by future generations or the degradation of ecosystem services caused by resource extraction. Export-oriented economies often fail to impose or enforce labor and environmental regulations in order to keep prices down. Wages, particularly in poor developing countries, are frequently inadequate to meet basic needs, and working conditions are often dangerous, debilitating, and degrading [108], contributing to a decline in workers' well-being [109]. We need to have effective labor and environmental policies in place that prevent the exploitation of foreign workers and internalize environmental costs. When we account for the real costs of labor, resource use, and externalities, then import prices will increase and the demand and consumption for these goods/services in rich countries will decrease. Also, the increase in labor wages will benefit the poor in developing countries, raising their purchasing power and improving their livelihoods [109]. High levels of consumption in rich countries may promote excessive resource degradation in poor countries, which jeopardizes well-being in the poorer countries.

Income inequality also drives excessive consumption. Once basic needs are met, relative income and status may be more important than total income. Consumption decisions are driven by comparisons with a reference group and the pursuit of status [109,110]. Status, however, requires consuming more status goods than one's peers and creates a never-ending treadmill. When the extremely wealthy spend more, less wealthy individuals on the fringes of their social circles also feel compelled to do so, followed by the even less well on the fringes of their circles, in what economist Robert Frank describes as an "expenditure cascade" [111]. In the presence of growing income inequality, this leads to a cycle of excessive work and indebtedness that can dramatically decrease quality of life. Partly as a result of the status treadmill, increases in labor productivity, education, skills, etc., have led to increases in production and consumption of goods and services, instead of more leisure time, earlier retirements, more holidays, etc.

Decreases in consumption in some goods and services can have rebound effects, leading to increases in consumption elsewhere [112]. For example, when people save money by driving a more fuel-efficient car or by increasing the energy efficiency of their homes, they may spend their savings on a holiday flight, resulting in a net increase in energy use [113]. Similar results can occur on larger scale, when increases in the efficiency of resource use lead to greater marginal benefits and an increase in total use [114]. In order to decrease consumption, all prices need to reflect real costs (environmental, social, and climate externalities). This will help achieve changes in consumption behavior and will limit, or even decrease, rebound effects. Policies should also target the composition of production and consumption to ensure that rebound effects are minimized. We can also decrease consumption through decreases in work time, which will translate into less purchasing power and thus less consumption and environmental degradation. By decreasing income and spending (income caps), it will also limit rebound effects [112,115]. However it does not guarantee a shift to cleaner consumption [112]. A cap-auction-trade scheme, rather than a tax, avoids the rebound effect by simply limiting quantity; any demand rebound just bids up price.

Improvements in technological efficiency are necessary, but not sufficient. They are more appealing to all because of their apolitical nature and mostly because they do not challenge production and consumption. However, there is an extensive literature showing how improvements in technological efficiency have led to increases in production and consumption due to a decrease in relative prices of products/services [72,109,115-117]. Some benefits of improvements in energy efficiency are offset by an increase in the demand for the product or service due to a decrease in price [116].

The increase in overall productivity through technological innovation has led to an increase in consumption and use of high quality energy and material resources, while avoiding the real social and environmental costs. Technological innovation also means a decrease in labor; the more efficient it becomes, the fewer workers are needed to produce the same level of outputs. This would work as long as the economy continues to grow and offsets labor productivity, but if there is a slowdown in the economy, then increasing productivity may also lead to increasing unemployment [118].

For many politicians, growth (increases in production and consumption) equals more jobs, thus attempts to decrease productivity growth are seen to reduce welfare [118]. However, decreases in productivity growth can be achieved by shifting from a product-based economy to a more service-based economy, since services are usually considered less material- and energy-intensive [118]. But it all depends on the type of services that are pursued; activities in the service sector can heavily depend on high levels of material and energy consumption (i.e., tourism and retail distribution). A focus on activities that promote social interaction and community engagement (farmers markets, crafts, community green projects, among others) will reduce labor productivity growth. The green service sector (less material and energy intensive) will also contribute to a reduction of GHG emissions [118].

We should also look at productivity growth as an opportunity for increasing leisure instead of consumption [109]. One approach to decreasing material and energy consumption is to reduce the time spent working. Less hours of work will limit production and consumption. Working less typically leads to reduced spending and also a shift to lower-impact forms of consumption: taking the bike instead of the car; cooking at home instead of buying fast food [119].

In addition, other regulations or policies that have been identified to decrease and/or reverse consumerism are:

• Taxing luxury consumption [16,115,120]: progressive taxes are necessary to disincentivize over-consumption, which has been pursued at the expense of increases in free time and environmental quality. For example, the book *Luxury Fever* has proposed a shift in the United States tax code to exempt savings and tax only consumption at very progressive rates [16]. Similarly, Howarth has proposed taxing status goods that increase energy and resource consumption [120]. Such policies could even benefit the rich by decreasing the level of consumption required to exhibit status, while leading to environmental benefits.

- Redirecting consumption from private status goods to public goods (investing in the commons), which will increase welfare [121]. Government can offer tax reductions or preferential investment conditions for activities that generate or protect public goods, such as green services to disincentivize energy and material intensive production and consumption. The rich could even benefit from higher taxes to fund these public goods: their status will be unaffected by across-the-board income reductions, while they will benefit from more public goods [122].

- Increasing employment in specific service sectors (health, green projects, community based projects, etc.) [115,123].

- Shifting the traditional focus of investment towards renewable energy, public goods, green (resource-efficient) technology, climate adaptation and mitigation, etc.

- Redistributing surpluses from private consumption to communal activities—urban food gardens, recycling, car-pooling—since communal activities tend to reduce conspicuous consumption.

- Incentivizing voluntary self-restrictions [115,124].

- Cap-and-auction policies for waste emissions that would internalize externalities and promote a shift towards cleaner consumption [112].

- Promoting and improving communication and the diffusion of information to reduce consumption, which would incentivize voluntary reductions in consumption and more socially desirable decisions; peer pressure plays a key role in consumption. This could be achieved by restoring the requirement for public service messages in exchange for private sector use of the airwaves.

- Directly controlling commercial advertising and media. The advertisement of status goods increases consumption since it encourages people to seek more income and to pursue wants that did not exist before. Regulation of advertising can lead to a change in individual/societal preferences [112,115]. Commercial advertising represents a social cost and the regulation of advertising will likely affect compositional consumption, increase well being, and decrease environmental degradation. Other measures might include banning advertising to children and in public spaces, establishing commercial-free zones and times, taxing advertising, and funding the right of reply to advertisers' claims [125,126]:

  * **Banning advertising in public spaces**: The Clean City Laws of São Paulo, Brazil. This law, introduced in 2007, completely bans outdoor advertising in the city and fines those who break it. The state of Vermont similarly bans billboards.

  * **Banning advertising for children**: Stockholm decided in 1991 to prohibit ads targeting children under 12 years. Greece does not allow war toy advertisements at all and any toy advertisements are prohibited between 7:00 AM and 10:00 PM. The U.K. does not allow the advertisement of alcohol to youths and requires ads to convey the size of the toys and what the toys can really do.

  * **Tax advertising**: Advertising is currently considered a business expense, exempt from taxation. This exemption should be removed, and an additional tax imposed on companies that spend more than a certain amount on advertising based on the rationale that advertising could be viewed as market externality that increases consumerism.

4.2. Expanding the Commons

To realize the transition to the new economic system we envision, it is necessary to greatly expand the commons sector of the economy, the sector responsible for managing existing common assets and creating new ones. Some assets, such as resources created by nature or by society as a whole, should be held in common because this is more just. Other assets, such as information or ecosystem structures (for example, forests), should be held in common because this is more efficient. Still other assets, such as essential common-pool resources and public goods, should be held in common because this is more sustainable.

One option for expanding and managing the commons sector is to create "common asset trusts" at various scales. Trusts, such as the Alaska Permanent Fund and regional land trusts, can propertize the commons without privatizing them [127]. Barnes [89] provides more specific examples of existing or proposed local, regional, national, and global initiatives for expanding the commons sector:

4.2.1. Local initiatives

a). **Land trusts**: There are various types of land trusts. One type is meant to protect land from development and degradation, which can be achieved via direct ownership of the land or by ownership of easements that restricts its use (e.g., the Marin Agricultural Land Trust, the Pacific Forest Trust, the Vermont Land Trust). Another type is meant to keep housing affordable. Land is held in a trust, while houses on the land are sold on the condition that the owner cannot profit from rising land values when the land is resold (e.g., the Champlain Housing Trust) [128,129].

b). **Conservation trusts**: Conservation funds for the protection of biodiversity that have been created since the 1990s through debt-swap funding or grants. These trusts were created with an endowment that allowed them to cover their short- and long-term needs (e.g., Bhutan Conservation Trust, The Mgahinga and Bwindy Impenetrable Forest Conservation Trust, and Colombian National Protected Areas Conservation Trust) [130].

c). **Terrestrial and marine protected areas**: Established for the protection and maintenance of biodiversity (marine sanctuaries, wildlife refuges, national parks, etc).

d). **Surface water trusts**: Acquisition of water rights to protect fish, other species, or aquatic ecosystems. This has also led to changes in agricultural practices like switching crops and changing irrigation patterns. A good example is the Oregon Water Trust.

e). **Groundwater trusts**: Permit issuance to limit the amount of water withdrawn from the aquifers, e.g., Edward Aquifer Authority in Texas.

f). **Community gardens**: Food production for neighborhoods and communities and promote community engagement.

g). **Farmers markets**: Commercial commons that provide fresh and local food, social interaction and engagement, awareness and importance of local produce, and other functions.

h). **Public spaces**: Spaces for social interaction that can be created by governments or reclaimed from urban spaces by neighbors or communities. Studies have shown that green public spaces can increase social inclusion for immigrant youth [131], protect against negative health impacts of stressful life events [132], and improve health overall and reduce income related health inequalities [133].

i). **Internet**: Using the Internet to remove communication barriers and improve democracy. Unlike television and other broadcast media, the Internet has very low technological and financial barriers for individuals seeking a presence there. This has the effect of decentralizing the production and distribution of information by returning control to the audience, providing a venue for dialogue instead of monologue. Opinions and services that were previously controlled by small groups or corporations are now shaped by the entire population. Television news networks, sitcoms, and Hollywood productions are being replaced by e-mail, Wikipedia, YouTube, and millions of blogs and forums—all created by the same millions of people who are the audience for the content [127].

4.2.2. Regional initiatives

a). **Air trusts**: An example of a regional air trust is the Regional Greenhouse Gas Initiative (RGGI), a cap-and-auction program in the U.S. Northeast, in which most revenues are dedicated to energy efficiency measures. This not only helps mitigate the distributional impacts by generating cost savings for households [134], but also helps to reduce GHG emissions far more than the caps themselves [135]. The European Union Emission Trading System is a cap-and-trade program that puts a cap on GHG emissions from businesses and creates a market for carbon allowances (UE Climate Action). However, most emission allowances are awarded directly to polluters, creating enormous windfall profits for firms. The goal, however, is to auction off half of emissions by 2013, which should help address this problem [136], and move towards the creation of common property rights to GHG absorption capacity. The United States cap-and-trade program for SO_2 emissions was successful at reducing pollution, but since it awarded emissions rights to polluters [137], it is really an example of the public sector transferring common assets to the private sector (which nonetheless may be superior than leaving them as open access resources).

b). **Watershed trusts**: To protect waterways, fish, and wildlife from agricultural run-off through the promotion of best management practices and sustainable agriculture. An example is the Southeastern Wisconsin Watersheds Trust for the Greater Milwaukee Watersheds.

c). **Land value tax**: These taxes capture some of the value of land for society as a whole, while providing numerous additional benefits. Harrisburg, Pennsylvania, for example, introduced a split tax on real estate, in which the tax on land far exceeded the tax on buildings. This made it necessary for owners of abandoned or degraded buildings to restore or replace them, in order to generate the income required to pay the tax, or sell the land to someone who would. The result was a revitalization of the urban center and an increase in its value as a public space.

d). **Buffalo Commons**: First proposed in 1987 for the social and ecological restoration of the Great Plains, the main purpose of the Commons is to re-establish a corridor between now-fragmented prairie lands for the bison and other wildlife to move freely along as well as to promote the health and sustainability of the land.

e). **Regional planning authorities**: These would begin to develop sustainable economic plans for regional implementation, building upon the lessons (positive and negative) of the Tennessee Valley Authority, the Appalachian Regional Commission, and numerous other modern regional efforts, including those in Canada, Australia, and within and between European Union member states such as in Torino, Ireland, and elsewhere [138-141].

4.2.3. National initiatives

a). **An American Permanent Fund**: The rationale for this fund would be similar to that of the Alaska Permanent Fund, i.e., to distribute common-property income equally to every citizen of the United States. Most of the income of the American Permanent Fund would originate from pollution permits (especially for CO_2), but also from the commons' share of corporate profit. The Fund would contribute to decreasing carbon emissions and improving overall well-being.

b). **Common tax credits**: The rationale behind this tax is that the wealthier segment of American society owes more to the commons than what they pay to the federal government in taxes. So government would increase taxes on the wealthier while giving them the option to either pay those taxes or contribute to a commons trust. An incentive to do the latter would be a 100-percent tax credit [89].

c). **National planning**: To help achieve local economic stability, to help distribute work and time in appropriate ways, and to manage potential dislocations caused by reduced growth.

4.2.4. Global initiatives

a). At a larger scale, a proposed Earth Atmospheric Trust could help to massively reduce global carbon emissions while also reducing poverty. This system would comprise a global cap-and-trade system for all greenhouse gas emissions (preferable to a tax, because it would set the quantity and allow price to vary); the auctioning of all emission permits before allowing trading among permit holders (to send the right price signals to emitters); and a reduction of the cap over time to stabilize atmospheric greenhouse gas concentrations at a level equivalent to 350 parts per million of carbon dioxide. The revenues resulting from these efforts would be deposited into the Earth Atmospheric Trust, administered transparently by trustees who serve long terms and have a clear mandate to protect earth's climate system and atmosphere for the benefit of current and future generations. A designated fraction of the revenues derived from auctioning the permits could then be returned to people throughout the world in the form of a per-capita payment. The remainder of the revenues could be used to enhance and restore the atmosphere, invest in social and technological innovations, assist developing countries, and administer the Trust [142].

b). International agreements are critical for the success of national climate policies and strategies. Through an international agreement, countries will not suffer for having strict national policies in place; they won't lose their comparative position. This will work in favor of the acceptability of the policies. As a result, there will be a shift toward clean, instead of dirty, production and consumption. It will also incentivize technological change [112].

c). A third possible global initiative is the "green paper gold" introduced by Joseph Stiglitz to promote investment in green infrastructure [143,144]. According to Stiglitz, green paper gold, also known as special drawing rights, are "a kind of global money, issued by the International Monetary Fund, which countries agree to exchange for dollars or other hard currencies." Stiglitz has argued that SDRs could be used to promote investment in the developing world and expanding the global commons or "global public goods" [144].

Government has a role to play in protecting and expanding the commons. When government is responsible for a common, it should act as its trustee and should be accountable for it. Government should also increase the allocation of property rights to commons trusts and contribute with the purchasing of former pieces of the commons, now privatized (e.g., through long-term tax-exempt bonds). Common asset trusts of the kind we have described are a mechanism for governments to fulfill these duties.

4.3. Implications of Systematic Caps on Natural Resources

A lasting prosperity requires much closer attention to the ecological limits of economic activity. Identifying and imposing strict resource and emission caps is vital for a sustainable economy. The contraction and convergence model developed for climate-related emissions should be applied more generally. Declining caps on throughput should be established for all non-renewable resources. Sustainable yields should be identified for renewable resources. Limits should be established for per-capita emissions and wastes. Effective mechanisms for imposing caps on these material flows should be set in place. Once established, these limits need to be built into the macro-economic frameworks.

Cap and Trade: Ownership of the quotas is initially public; the government auctions them to individuals and firms. The revenues go to the treasury and could be used to replace regressive taxes, such as the payroll tax, and to reduce income tax on the lowest incomes, or else to increase investments in public goods or energy efficiency measures that benefit the poor. Once purchased at auction, the quotas can be freely bought and sold by third parties, just as can the resources whose rate of depletion they limit. The trading allows efficient allocation, the auction serves just distribution, and the cap serves the goal of sustainable scale. However, free trading threatens speculative investments and other forms of gaming the market to capture rent. More frequent auctions of permits that could not subsequently be traded could avoid this risk. The same logic can be applied to limiting the off-take from fisheries and forests. With renewables, the quota should be set to approximate sustainable yield. For nonrenewables, sustainable rates of absorption of resulting pollution or the rate of development of renewable substitutes may provide a criterion [80]. It's worth noting that in a survey conducted in Vermont, only 5.8 percent of respondents favored distributed revenue equally among households; 64.2 percent favored investing it in natural resources, 14.2 percent favored investing it public goods such as education and healthcare, and the remainder favored some mix of dividends and public investments [145].

The idea of a carbon tax and other pollution taxes as a replacement for payroll taxes has gotten political support. It has been recognized that it makes more sense to tax what we burn instead of what we earn [146]. A very popular method, the Alaskan Permanent Fund, pays a dividend to the citizens of Alaska from the fossil fuel revenue the state collects [146]. This model is known as "cap and dividend," "where some fraction of the revenues of an auction on emissions allowance is returned to citizens on an equal per capita basis" [147]. However, in the case of fossil fuel use, where prices are determined at the global level, and not influenced by extraction rates in any single state, this leads to citizen pressure to "drill, baby, drill," increasing outputs and revenue. In the case of cap and auctions on emissions, local caps would determine prices. Given the highly inelastic demand for fossil fuels (and hence for the waste absorption capacity for CO_2), the tighter the cap, the greater the total revenue, since every 1-percent restriction in quantity would lead to a greater than 1-percent increase in price.

Cap and dividend is considered by some to be a fair and transparent model, since it is based on the amount of carbon-based energy a person consumes. The more a person consumes, the more he/she would have to pay. It would also have a progressive distributional effect; poor people usually consume less energy than the middle class and the rich [147]. For cap and dividend to work, there would have to be a cap on fossil fuel supplies. It is much easier and more cost-effective to have an economy-wide cap on suppliers than emitters. Companies that sell fossil fuel would have to buy permits equal to the carbon content of the fuels they sell. Then, once a year there would be an auditing to make sure the companies have enough permits; if they don't, they would have to pay a high penalty. The number of permits would be reduced every year, decreasing the amount of carbon that enters the economy. As the carbon cap declined, prices would increase and private capital would shift to cleaner alternative technologies and cleaner production and consumption.

Another important element of this model is the dividend, which would be paid equally to every American once a month. As carbon prices increase, so would the dividend, and this in turn would increase the livelihoods of the poor [146,147].

However, from a global perspective, a cap and dividend regime in the United States or other wealthy country may be unfair. Both Europe's existing cap and any of the proposed caps in the United States far exceed a fair share of global absorption capacity, and completely fail to account for past contributions to the carbon stock. As discussed previously, reducing flows to ecologically sustainable levels in the short run would likely cause economic collapse, with the worst impacts likely to be borne by the poor. Perhaps the most sustainable, fair, and efficient approach would be for rich countries to invest revenue in making existing infrastructure more energy efficient, and in investing in new, open-source technologies for alternative energy and energy efficiency. This would be more sustainable since it would accelerate the rate at which we develop new technologies and reduce emissions; it would be more fair because it would put the burden of developing new technologies on the wealthy countries, and because the poor would likely benefit most from more energy efficient housing and infrastructure; and it would be more efficient because information is non-rival and should therefore be open access to all, which requires public sector investment, as explained above. Currently, the United States energy sector invests only 0.03 percent of sales in R&D, which is clearly inadequate given the importance of developing low carbon energy [148].

A variation on the cap-auction-trade mechanism is the commons asset trust, for example, the Earth Atmospheric Trust described above [90]. In this mechanism, as in the cap-auction-trade, caps are established around a resource. However, in this case a trust manages the sale of permits and the revenue from the auction. It can adjust the availability of permits, depending on need, though ultimately resource use cannot exceed planetary boundaries. The trust would provide equal dividends to the citizens (in a national system) or to countries for distribution to their populations (in an international system), or else invest revenues in public goods. The benefit of providing dividends directly to the population is that it provides some mitigation to the inevitable price increases passed down to consumers [146]. However, households and businesses frequently fail to adopt energy efficiency measures with high rates of return [149]. This may be especially true for poor households that lack the resources, knowledge, and initiative required to undertake such investments. Recycling revenue into energy efficiency investments with high rates of return would effectively increase total benefits, and could therefore benefit poor households even more than dividends.

An alternative and intermediate option is also available by returning some fraction of the annual revenues as dividends to the population, but using the remainder for other purposes related to preserving and enhancing the common assets, such as atmosphere and climate. This would allow for rewarding people that have a lower carbon footprint to be rewarded as well as for providing funds for related projects like researching and developing renewable energy, deploying renewable energy technologies in developing countries, paying for ecosystem services like carbon sequestration, etc. [142].

National environmental policies nearly all result in internalizing previously uncounted ecological and social costs. This naturally increases prices relative to those in countries that do not internalize these costs, putting domestic firms at a competitive disadvantage in international trade if the country's international policy is free trade. In this case national and international policies are inconsistent. An international policy consistent with national cost internalization would require moving away from free trade by imposing cost-equalizing tariffs on imports produced under conditions that do not internalize these costs. This is protection, to be sure—but it is protection of an efficient national policy of cost internalization, not protection of an inefficient national firm. Without such protection, or international agreement on cost-internalizing measures, there would be a competitive, cost-externalizing race to the bottom. Globalization (free trade coupled with free capital mobility) seeks to substitute the transnational corporation for the nation as the controlling economic power. Existing traditional community at the national level is sacrificed to the abstraction of a very tenuous "global community."

4.4. Sharing Work Time

We need labor policies that allow and encourage shorter work time. Reductions in work time are one of the most cited policies to sustain full employment (or at least decrease unemployment) without increasing output, and to protect workers' livelihoods [72,112,119].

Work-share programs are considered one of the best ways to respond to a short-term decrease in economic activity. Sharing work time can help reduce, and even prevent, layoffs and also serve as a stabilizer when the economy is slow or the country is facing an imminent recession. Work-share programs help avoid re-hiring and re-training costs and would work best if implemented during the early months of the economic downturn [119]. In the United States, work sharing has helped save jobs. In 2009, work sharing saved 166,000 jobs, three times more than in 2008. Jack Reid, the Democratic senator from Rhode Island, has introduced work-share bills in Congress (in 2009 and 2010) in an effort to encourage more states to implement such programs. Currently 20 states across the United States operate work-share programs [119].

Shorter working hours will improve the work-life balance. Having more time to spend with family and engaging in social interactions has been found to increase subjective well-being, which could lead to decreases in consumption [150-152]. Some of the benefits of shorter work hours are less stress and work pressure as well as more time for activities like gardening, child care, meals, volunteer work, social interactions, and so on [150]. Kasser and Brown found that people with more leisure time have a smaller ecological footprint [151]. Schor also found similar results: there is a significant positive correlation between work hours and the ecological footprint [73].

There are different types of hours reduction that can be used: reduced average hours per job, reduced average annual hours per person, shorter total hours per working life, etc. The different types of hour reduction will have diverse welfare and economic impacts, which is why it is important to have a just distribution of hours to ensure political feasibility in the long run. Ultimately, environmental degradation will depend on total number of hours worked per capita, which is a function of average hours per job per person and the employment-to-population ratio [73].

Increases in productivity of capital and labor can be accomplished through increases in production and consumption, increases in leisure, or a combination of the two. Thus a greater proportion of any future gains in productivity being taken as an increase in leisure will decrease the rate of unemployment and reduce environmental degradation [121]. The shift to policies that channel productivity growth into increases in free time instead of increases in income will impact the product mix and/or the composition of consumption and can increase environmental degradation because of time-use rebound effects. According to a study on the household production function, time-saving innovations in the production of a service result in an increase in the demand for that service. If the service is energy intensive (i.e., transportation), then the energy demand will increase [73,153]. Thus, the time-use rebound effect will depend on the type of activity that increases as work hours are reduced and there is more free time available. At the household level, families with more purchasing power and less time will invest in time-saving activities, products such as faster transportation and fast food, which are both more energy intensive and require less time [154].

From the production side, if the economy is slowing down (decreases in GDP) or going into recession, it would be necessary to reduce work hours in order to decrease or even avoid unemployment (assuming increases in population). From the consumption side, keeping or increasing work hours will lead to increases in productivity growth (GDP growth), which is translated into increased income and consumption [116]. Working hours affect income and fuel the spending culture, which Knight and colleagues have called the "work and spend" cycle [116]. When a society is in a "work and spend" cycle, advertising and marketing are more effective in promoting consumption. Furthermore, the increases in productivity growth, translated into increases in production and consumption, lead to increases in environmental degradation.

Society has been focusing on green and more efficient technology to decrease energy consumption and GHG emissions, however technological efficiency is necessary but not sufficient. Consumption, energy use, and GHG emissions are closely interconnected and depend on how increasing productivity is achieved, through increases in income or through decreases in work hours. Nässén and colleagues analyzed the income effect of shorter working hours and how consumption and energy use is affected, and found a strong relationship between income and energy use [155]. Thus a decrease in work time/income of 1 percent leads to a decrease in energy use of 0.89 percent. However, when analyzing the time effect of shorter work hours—how changes in work hours affect time use off work and, in turn, energy use—the results show that a decrease in work hours by 1 percent leads to an increase in energy use of o.06 percent and a respective increase in CO_2 of 0.02 percent. If we calculate the net effect of both, the sum of income and time effects, shorter work hours will lead to decreases in energy use of .83 percent and decreases in CO_2 of 0.85 percent [155]. Rosnick and Weisbrot found the same positive significant relationship between work hours and energy use [156]. They showed that a 1-percent increase in work hours per worker increased energy use by 1.32 percent (controlling for GDP/hour, worker/population, and temperature). They estimated that if European Union workers worked as many hours as U.S. workers, there would be an 18 percent increase in energy consumption in the European Union.

Schor argues that there are four main barriers/challenges related to labor costs that disincentivize firms to support decreases in work hours [73]:

a). Firms increase wages above market clearing levels to raise the cost of job loss. Thus longer working hours lead to increases in the cost of job loss.

b). Employment related costs (hiring costs, training costs, fringe benefits, etc.) are structured based on the worker and not on hours worked.

c). Workers paid annual salaries instead of per-hour wages tend to work more. Schor found that working for an annual salary instead of a per-hour salary increases the number of work hours up to 100–150 per year [73].

d). An upward-sloping labor supply function will cause the firm to prefer longer hours to avoid salary increases or decreases in worker quality.

Many firms also do not take into consideration workers' preferences for shorter hours. Thus, ion contrast to what the dominant paradigm of neoclassical economics states, workers do not prefer to work more to increase future income and hence consumption. On the contrary, according to several studies [116,157], workers are willing to forgo future increases in income in exchange for a reduction in work hours, since future income is less valued. For example, using International Social Survey Programme survey data for 21 developed countries, Otterbach and Sanne showed evidence indicating that, in countries with higher GDP, people prefer to work less even if this means earning less income [157,158]. However, it is important to note that workers are averse to decreases in present income because of habit formation (preferences adapt to current income and consumption levels). Furthermore, firms that do allow shorter work hours can, and many times do, penalize workers for choosing them by denying medical insurance, pensions, opportunity for career trajectory jobs or promotions, and so on [73].

Surveys done before the 2008 crash indicate that 30–50 percent of Americans expressed a preference for fewer work hours, even for less pay [159]. Germany responded to the 2008 crash primarily through the adjustment of hours, and as a result unemployment rates barely increased. This was achieved through the combination of a federal scheme to replace lost wages (which accounted for about 20 percent of the reduction in hours), private bargains between employers and unions, canceled overtime, and flexible use of vacation and other time off [159]. There has also been an increase in leisure time in various OECD countries [118].

General policies that would help achieve shorter working hours include:

1. Compensation for reducing working time: a package deal to receive compensation for reducing or sharing work hours [106].

2. Limiting overtime through disincentives to employees and/or raising the overtime premium to make it more expensive for firms to use overtime [106,150]. High levels and increases in income inequality have been identified as one of the reasons workers prefer to work longer hours [75].

3. Standardizing working hours and building flexibility for workers into the labor economy [112,119]. Examples of the latter might include:

a). A federal law that allows shorter hours of work to be compensated through at least partial unemployment insurance, to offset the forgone income. States now have the option under federal law to apply for this but many have not done so.

b). Government hiring on an 80-percent schedule. Government is a big employer and this would have a ripple effect. Policymakers could also structure tax credits to give incentives to employers who hire on 80-percent schedules, which would enable more people to be brought back into the labor force than if hiring were done on the full-time schedule.

4. Promoting self-employment and considering adopting the Danish example of "flexicuity" (a combination of flexibility in the labor market, protection for the self-employed, and labor market policy) [106].

5. Structurally restricting the flow of increased future income in order to reduce consumption. People are more willing to forgo future increases in income and consumption than cuts in current income and consumption [73].

6. As for firms, some incentives that would encourage the firm to accept shorter work time include [73]:

a). Removing the firms' upper-limit payments to social welfare funds.

b). Shifting the responsibility for social welfare to outside entities, like unions, the state, etc. In some cases it may help to create a market for hours, so unions can bargain for workers.

c). Ensuring cost-neutral work time reductions through the provision of state subsidies to compensate the firm or through the structure of the deals that are struck with the workers.

7. Transforming a percentage of future productivity gains into shorter work time, but for a large part of the population and not just for a some workers [155].

8. Ensuring basic citizens' income to help equalize wages/income disparities and ensure that workers would be more willing to reduce work hours [118].

9. Increasing diversity in labor contracts to allow for shorter work time, early retirement, regular sabbaticals, etc., and at the same time ensuring pension systems as safety nets for workers.

5. Are These Policies Consistent and Feasible?

We have so far presented a brief vision of what a sustainable and desirable "ecological economy" would look like, and a summary list of some of the policies we think would be required in order to get there. This begs the important question of whether these policies taken together are consistent and whether they are sufficient to achieve the goals we have articulated. Can we have a global economy that is not growing in material terms but that is sustainable and provides a high quality of life for most (if not all) people? While we can never really know the answer to this question until we actually try it out in practice, we can provide a few lines of evidence to help anticipate whether such an economy-in-society-in-nature can work. These include lessons from history, modern day small-scale examples, and modeling studies. We will briefly discuss each of these lines of evidence in turn.

5.1. Lessons from History[1]

Human history has traditionally been cast in terms of the rise and fall of great civilizations, wars, specific human achievements, and extreme natural disasters (e.g., earthquakes, floods, plagues). This history tends to leave out, however, the important ecological and climatic context and the less obvious interactions which shaped and mediated these events. The capability to integrate human history with new data about the natural history of the earth at global scales and over centuries to millennia has only recently become possible. It is a critical missing link that is needed in order to provide a much richer picture of how (and why) the planet has changed in historical times, and how (and why) past human societies have either been able to sustain themselves or have collapsed.

Socio-ecological systems are intimately linked in ways that we are only beginning to appreciate [160-163]. One major challenge in linking human and environmental change is the development of a new integrated analytical modeling paradigm that reveals the complex web of causation across multiple spatial and temporal scales, while allowing important emergent properties and generalities to rise above the details. Only with such a paradigm can we survey the past and test alternate explanations rigorously. To develop this integrated understanding, a project of the global change research community has been initiated, titled Integrated History and Future of People on Earth (IHOPE) [164].

The big, general questions that the IHOPE activity is aimed at addressing can be summarized as the following:

1. What are the complex and interacting mechanisms and processes resulting in the emergence, sustainability, or collapse of socio-ecological systems?

2. What are the pathways to developing and evaluating alternative explanatory frameworks, specific explanations, and models (including complex systems models) by using observations of highly variable quality and coverage?

---

1 This section relies heavily on Costanza, Graumlich, et al. 2007.

3. How do we use knowledge of the integrated history of the earth for understanding and creating the future?

It has often been said that if one fails to understand the past, one is doomed to repeat it. IHOPE takes a much more "hopeful" and positive attitude. If we can really understand the past, we can create a better, more sustainable, and desirable future.

Getting back to the original intention of this section, we can ask: Have there ever been non-growing economies that have been sustainable? Actually, this question needs to be turned around, since for the vast majority of human history, economies have grown at very low to zero rates. If anything, from an historical perspective, it is the phenomenal rate of growth of recent economies that is the anomaly. However, we also know that many historical societies have collapsed [12,163] and many of them were not what we would call "desirable." On the other hand, there were a few successful historical cases in which decline did not occur, including the following [163,165]:

*   Tikopia Islanders have maintained a sustainable food supply and non-increasing population with a bottom-up social organization.
*   New Guinea features a silviculture system more than 7,000 years old with an extremely democratic, bottom-up decision-making structure.
*   Japan's top-down forest and population policies in the Tokugawa-era arose as a response to an environmental and population crisis, bringing an era of stable population, peace, and prosperity.

Understanding the history of how humans have interacted with the rest of nature can help clarify the options for managing our increasingly interconnected global system. However, we know from history that non-growing societies are feasible. We also know that sustainable societies are possible. As we learn more about the details of historical societies' interaction with the rest of nature, we can use that knowledge to help design a better, more sustainable, and desirable future.

5.2. Small-Scale Examples

There are many small-scale examples of sustainable communities that can serve as models. Many groups and communities around the world are involved in building a new economic vision and testing solutions. There are far too many to list all, but here are a few examples:

*   Transition town movement (http://www.transitionnetwork.org)
*   Global EcoVillage Network (http://gen.ecovillage.org)
*   Co-Housing Network (http://www.cohousing.org/)
*   Wiser Earth (http://www.wiserearth.org)
*   Sustainable Cities International (http://www.sustainablecities.net)
*   Center for a New American Dream (http://www.newdream.org)
*   Democracy Collaborative (http://www.community-wealth.org)
*   Portland, Oregon, Bureau of Planning and Sustainability (http://www.portlandonline.com/bps/index.cfm)

All of these examples embody the vision, worldview, and policies we have elaborated to some extent. Their experiments collectively provide evidence that the policies are feasible at a smaller scale. The challenge is to scale up some of these models to society as a whole.

The problem is that we live in a globalized world and it is difficult to generate larger scale examples that are independent enough from the world to actually try something significantly different. In a sense, we need a total "regime shift" to a new system [42] and that often requires at least a partial collapse of the existing order.

Nevertheless, even though the world is still largely enmeshed in the conventional economic paradigm, several cities, states, regions, and countries are further along the path we outline than others. Examples include Portland, Oregon; Stockholm and Malmö, Sweden; London, U.K.; the states of Vermont, Washington, and Oregon in the U.S.; Germany, Sweden, Iceland, Denmark, Costa Rica, Bhutan; and many others.

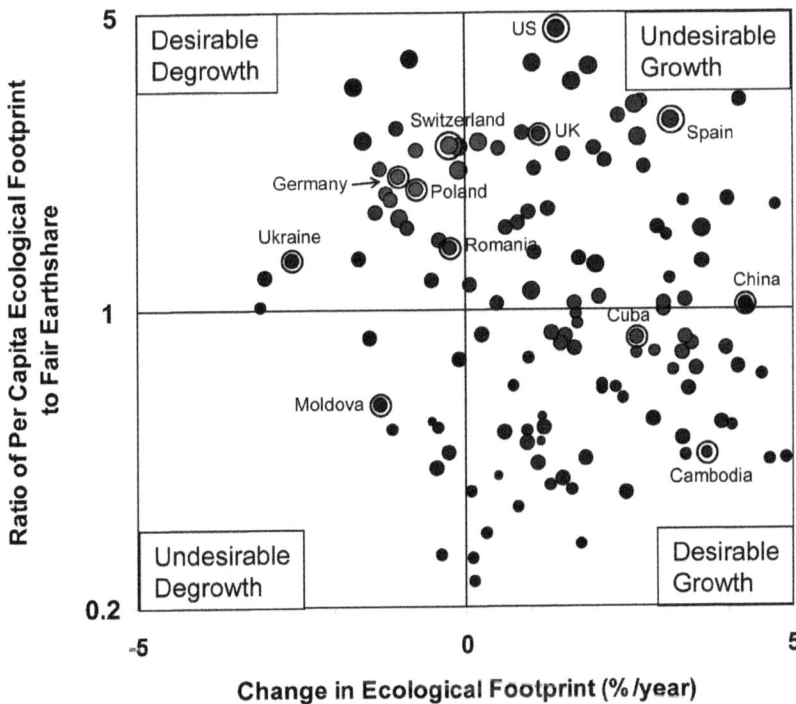

Figure 9. Relationship between change in ecological footprint and distance from per-capita biocapacity by country [166].

One way to look at this transition is shown in Figure 9, which plots the percent change in ecological footprint by country (an indicator of change in material and energy throughput) against per-capita fair share of the ecological footprint relative to global bio-capacity (an indicator of the scale of the economy, with 1 indicating "optimal" scale) [166]. This divides the graph into four quadrants, with the center of the graph representing countries that are closest to steady state. In the upper right quadrant are countries whose ecological footprint is increasing and is above their optimal scale. This is "undesirable growth." In the upper left quadrant are countries that are still above their optimal scale but whose ecological footprint is decreasing. This is "desirable degrowth." Likewise, countries that are below their optimal scale are either experiencing "undesirable degrowth" if their ecological footprint is decreasing or "desirable growth" if their footprint is increasing.

The policies we have recommended in this report would drive countries toward the center of this graph. Depending on the country, this could involve either growth or degrowth of material and energy throughput and the scale of the economy, accompanied by an improvement in human well-being broadly defined.

The transition to the world we envision will be a process of directed cultural evolution [42]. To direct this process, we need to generate, communicate, and broadly discuss more smaller-scale experiments that embody the vision and policies we have articulated.

However, a third line of evidence for the feasibility of our vision is based on *simulating* how these societies might work.

5.3. Modeling Studies

There are several integrated modeling studies that provide evidence that a sustainable, non-growing economy is both feasible and desirable. Below we briefly describe three of them.

5.3.1. World3[2]

The World3 model has been the subject of three influential books, beginning with *The Limits to Growth* [168], continuing with *Beyond the Limits* [169] and ending with the recent, 30-year update [170]. World3 is a globally aggregated systems dynamics model broken into five sectors: population, capital, agriculture, nonrenewable resources, and persistent pollution, and containing 16 state variables (i.e., population, capital, pollution, and arable land), 100 variables total, and 80 fixed parameters [168].

Because of the influence of the original book (several million copies were sold), this model has been the topic of intense scrutiny, debate, misunderstanding, and, one could argue, willful misinformation over the years. One interesting bit of misinformation that has been persistently circulating is the idea that the model's "predictions" have been proven totally wrong by subsequent events [171]. In fact, the model's standard run scenario, made in 1972, fits the data so far very well [172]. The model's forecasts of collapse under certain scenarios did not start to occur until well past the year 2000. The true tests of this model's forecasts will arrive in the coming decades.

World3 has been criticized on methodological grounds [173]. The most often cited difficulties are that it does not include prices explicitly, that it assumes resources are ultimately limited, and that it does not present estimates of the statistical uncertainty of its parameters. In fact, World3 is a viable and effective method to reveal the implications of the primary assumptions about the nature of the world that went into it. That is all that can be claimed for any model. These assumptions, or "pre-analytic visions," need to be made clear and placed in direct comparison with the corresponding assumptions of the alternatives, in this case the "unlimited growth model." As Meadows and colleagues have

---

2 This and the following section are adapted from 167. Costanza R, Leemans R, Boumans R, Gaddis E (2007) Integrated global models. In: Costanza R, Graumlich L, Steffen W, editors. Sustainability or collapse? An integrated history and future of people on earth. Cambridge, MA: MIT Press. pp. 417-446.

repeatedly pointed out, the essential difference in pre-analytic visions centers around the existence and role of limits: thermodynamic limits, natural resource limits, pollution absorption limits, population carrying capacity limits, and most importantly, the limits of our understanding about where these limits are and how they influence the system [169,170]. The alternative unlimited growth model assumes there are no limits that cannot be overcome by continued technological progress, while the limited growth model assumes that there are limits, based on thermodynamic first principles, observations of natural ecosystems, and understanding of basic planetary boundaries [1]. Ultimately, we do not know which pre-analytic vision is correct (they are, after all, assumptions), so we have to consider the relative costs of being wrong in each case [37,174].

Finally, while the discussions of World3 often point to the limited vs. unlimited growth assumptions as a key difference from conventional economic models, they do not take the opportunity to look at the relative costs and benefits of being right or wrong in those assumptions. If one does this, one can easily see that the cost of assuming no limits and being wrong is the collapse scenarios shown by World3, while the cost of assuming limits and being wrong is only mildly constrained growth [174].

5.3.2. GUMBO

The Global Unified Metamodel of the BiOsphere (GUMBO) [175] was developed by a working group at the National Center for Ecological Analysis and Synthesis (NCEAS) in Santa Barbara, California. Its goal was to simulate the integrated earth system and assess the dynamics and values of ecosystem services. It is a "metamodel" in that it represents a synthesis and a simplification of several existing dynamic global models in both the natural and social sciences at an intermediate level of complexity. GUMBO is the first global model to include the dynamic feedbacks among human technology, economic production and welfare, and ecosystem goods and services within the dynamic earth system. GUMBO includes five distinct modules or "spheres": the atmosphere, lithosphere, hydrosphere, biosphere, and anthroposphere. The earth's surface is further divided into 11 biomes or ecosystem types, which encompass the entire surface area of the planet: open ocean, coastal ocean, forests, grasslands, wetlands, lakes/rivers, deserts, tundra, ice/rock, croplands, and urban. The relative areas of each biome change in response to urban and rural population growth, gross world product (GWP), and changes in global temperature. Among the spheres and biomes, there are exchanges of energy, carbon, nutrients, water, and mineral matter. In GUMBO, ecosystem services are aggregated to seven major types, while ecosystem goods are aggregated into four major types. Ecosystem services, in contrast to ecosystem goods, cannot accumulate or be used at a specified rate of depletion. Ecosystem services include soil formation, gas regulation, climate regulation, nutrient cycling, disturbance regulation, recreation and culture, and waste assimilation. Ecosystem goods include water, harvested organic matter, mined ores, and extracted fossil fuel. These 11 goods and services represent the output from natural capital, which combines with built capital, human capital, and social capital to produce economic goods and services and social welfare. The model calculates the marginal product of ecosystem services in both the production and welfare functions as estimates of the shadow prices of each service.

Historical calibrations from 1900 to 2000 for 14 key variables for which quantitative time series data were available produced an average R^2 of 0.922. A range of future scenarios to the year 2100 representing different assumptions about future technological change, investment strategies, and other factors have been simulated. The scenarios include a base case (using the "best fit" values of the model parameters over the historical period) and four initial alternative scenarios. These four alternatives are the result of two variations (a technologically optimistic set and a skeptical set) concerning assumptions about key parameters in the model, arrayed against two variations (a technologically optimistic and a skeptical set) of policy settings concerning the rates of investment in the four types of capital (natural, social, human, and built). They correspond to the four scenarios laid out by Costanza [37] and are very similar to the four scenarios used in the Millennium Ecosystem Assessment [17].

Like World3, GUMBO can produce scenarios of global steady state or overshoot and decline. Achieving a steady state is possible with investment and population priorities similar to the ones outlined in the previous sections of this report, indicating that the policies are internally consistent.

5.3.3. LowGrow[3]

More recently, the "LowGrow" model of the Canadian economy has been used to describe the possibility of constructing an economy that is not growing in GDP terms but that is stable, with high employment, low carbon emissions, and high quality of life [121,176]. LowGrow was explicitly constructed as a fairly conventional macroeconomic model calibrated for the Canadian economy, with added features to simulate the effects on natural and social capital. Figure 10 shows the simplified structure of LowGrow. Aggregate (macro) demand is determined in the normal way as the sum of consumption expenditure (C), investment expenditure (I), government expenditure (G), and the difference between exports (X) and imports (I.) Their sum total is GDP measured as expenditure. There are separate equations for each of these components in the model, estimated with Canadian data from about 1981 to 2005, depending on the variable. Production in the economy is estimated by a Cobb-Douglas production function in which macro supply is a function of employed labor (L) and employed capital (K). The time variable (t) represents changes in productivity from improvements in technology, labor skills, and organization. The production function is shown as macro supply at the bottom of Figure 10. It estimates the labor (L) and employed capital (K) required to produce GDP allowing for changes in productivity over time.

There is a second important link between aggregate demand and the production function. Investment expenditures (net of depreciation), which are part of aggregate demand, add to the economy's stock of capital, increasing its productive capacity. Also, capital and labor become more productive over time. It follows that, other things equal, without an increase in aggregate demand these increases in capital and productivity reduce employment. Economic growth (i.e., increases in GDP) is needed to prevent unemployment rising as capacity and productivity increase.

Population is determined exogenously in LowGrow, which offers a choice of three projections from Statistics Canada. Population is also one of the variables that determines consumption expenditures in the economy. The labor force is estimated in LowGrow as a function of GDP and population.

There is no monetary sector in LowGrow. For simplicity it is assumed that the Bank of Canada, Canada's central bank, regulates the money supply to keep inflation at or near the target level of 2 percent per year. LowGrow includes an exogenously set rate

---

3 Adapted from 176. Victor PA (2008) Managing without growth: slower by design, not disaster. Cheltenham, UK: Edward Elgar Publishing.

of interest that remains unchanged throughout each run of the model. A higher cost of borrowing discourages investment, which reduces aggregate demand. It also raises the cost to the government of servicing its debt.

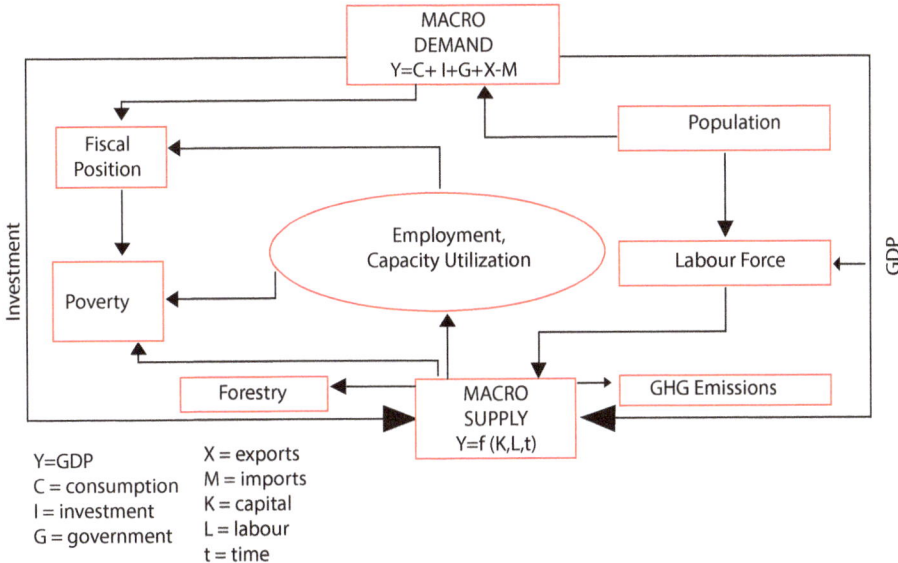

Figure 10. The high level structure of LowGrow [176].

The price level is not included as a variable in LowGrow, although the model warns of inflationary pressures when the rate of unemployment falls below 4 percent (effectively full employment in Canada).

LowGrow includes features that are particularly relevant for exploring a low/no-growth economy. LowGrow includes emissions of carbon dioxide and other greenhouse gases, a carbon tax, a forestry sub-model, and provision for redistributing incomes. It measures poverty using the UN's Human Poverty Index (i.e., HPI-2 for selected OECD countries). LowGrow allows additional funds to be spent on health care and on programs for reducing adult illiteracy (both included in HPI-2) and estimates their impacts on longevity and adult literacy with equations from the literature.

Implications of changes in the level of government expenditures can be simulated in LowGrow through a variety of fiscal policies, including an annual percentage change in government expenditure that can vary over time, and a balanced budget. LowGrow keeps track of the overall fiscal position of all three levels of government combined (federal, provincial, and municipal) by calculating total revenues and expenditures and estimating debt repayment based on the historical record. As the level of government indebtedness declines, the rates of taxes on personal incomes and profits in LowGrow are reduced endogenously, broadly consistent with government policy in Canada.

In LowGrow, as in the economy that it represents, economic growth is driven by net investment (which adds to productive assets), growth in the labor force, increases in productivity, growth in the net trade balance, growth in government expenditures, and growth in population. Low- and no-growth scenarios can be examined by reducing the rates of increase in each of these factors singly or in combination.

Economic growth is desired not only for what it offers in terms of increased living standards but also out of fear of what might happen if a modern economy deliberately tried to wean itself off growth. Such fears are well-founded. Modern economies and their public, private, and not-for-profit institutions, as well as individual citizens, have come to rely on growth. They expect it, they plan for it, they believe in it.

Several scenarios have been run with LowGrow to look at the feasibility of a low- or no-growth economy. Adjusting to life without economic growth could be a wrenching experience and a lot could go wrong, as shown in Figure 11. In this scenario, zero growth in GDP and GDP per capita is achieved around 2030 by eliminating growth in government expenditures, productivity, and population, and achieving zero net investment and net trade balance over a period of years starting in 2010. GDP per capita rises slightly until all the factors contributing to growth are extinguished and then drops back to the same level as at the start of 2005. Meanwhile, the unemployment rate literally goes off the chart, causing a dramatic rise in poverty. The debt-to-GDP ratio also rises to untenable heights, largely because of the massive increase in income support paid to the rising number of unemployed. Certainly, the human misery entailed in such a scenario is to be avoided if at all possible (Figure 11).

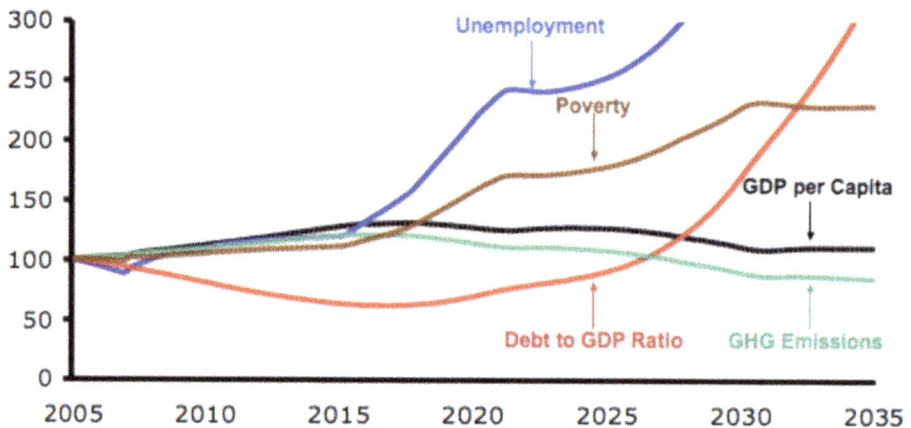

Figure 11. A no-growth disaster [176].

However, a wide range of low- and no-growth scenarios can be examined with LowGrow. Some are not much better than the no-growth disaster just described, but others offer more promise. One such promising scenario is shown in Figure 12.

Compared with the business as usual scenario, GDP per capita grows more slowly, leveling off around 2028, at which time the rate of unemployment is 5.7 percent. The unemployment rate continues to decline to 4.0 percent by 2035. By 2020 the poverty index declines from 10.7 to an internationally unprecedented level of 4.9, where it remains, and the debt-to-GDP ratio declines to about 30 percent and is maintained at that level to 2035. Greenhouse gas emissions are 31 percent lower at the start of 2035 than 2005 and 41 percent lower than their high point in 2010. These results are obtained by slower growth in government expenditures, net investment, and productivity; a positive net trade balance; cessation of growth in population; a reduced workweek; a revenue-neutral carbon tax; and increased government expenditure on anti-poverty programs, adult literacy programs, and health care.

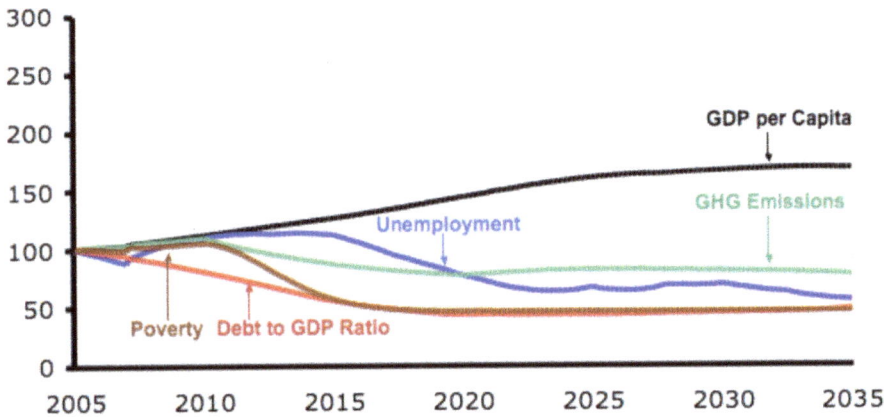

Figure 12. A better low/no growth scenario [176].

The contrast between the no-growth disaster (Figure 11) and the sustainable and desirable no-growth scenario (Figure 12) is striking and naturally raises questions about what makes the difference. The no-growth disaster scenario is based on a systematic elimination of all of the factors represented in LowGrow that contribute to growth without any compensating adjustments. The better no/low-growth scenario results from a wide range of policy measures, some more controversial than others, that would be required to transform the business as usual scenario into the kind of scenario illustrated in Figure 12. In summary, these policy measures include:

- **Investment**: reduced net investment, a shift from investment in private to public goods through changes in taxation and expenditures.
- **Labor force**: stabilization through changing age structure of the population and population stabilization.
- **Population**: stabilization through changes to immigration policy.
- **Poverty**: trickle down replaced with focused anti-poverty programs that address the social determinants of illness and provide more direct income support.
- **Technological change**: slower, more discriminating, and preventative rather than end-of-pipe, through technology assessment and changes in the education of scientists and engineers.
- **Government expenditures**: a declining rate of increase.
- **Trade**: a stable, positive net trade balance (and diversification of markets).
- **Work week**: shorter and with more leisure, through changes in compensation, work organization and standard working hours, and active market labor policies.
- **Greenhouse gases**: a revenue neutral carbon tax.

To complement these policies:

- Consumption: more public goods and fewer positional (status) goods, through changes in taxation and marketing.
- Environment and resources: limits on throughput and use of space through better land use planning and habitat protection and ecological fiscal reform.
- Localization: fiscal and trade policies to strengthen local economies.

These are precisely the policies that we have elaborated in the previous sections of this report. No model results can be taken as definitive, since models are only as good as the assumptions that go into them. But what World3, GUMBO, and LowGrow have provided is some evidence for the *consistency* and *feasibility* of these policies, taken together, to produce an economy that is not growing in GDP terms, but that is sustainable and desirable.

6. Conclusions

The world is at a critical turning point. This turning will not come overnight, however. In fact we are probably already in the middle of it. It will take decades. But it is a time of real choices: (1) we can attempt to continue business as usual, pursuing the conventional economic growth paradigm that has dominated economic policy since the end of World War II; (2) we can pursue an environmentally sensitive version of this model and attempt to achieve "green growth"; or (3) we can pursue a more radical departure from the mainstream that does not consider growth to be the real goal at all, but rather sustainable human well-being, acknowledging uncertainty and the complexity of understanding, creating, and sustaining well-being (Table 1). This report has described option 3, which entails a change in worldview, vision, and goals that would have far-reaching implications and will demand a substantial departure from business as usual. However, we believe it is the only option that is both sustainable and desirable on our finite planet.

In this report we have sketched a vision of what this "ecological economics" option might look like and how we could get there. We believe that this option can provide full employment and a high quality of life for everyone into the indefinite future while staying within the safe environmental operating space for humanity on earth. Developed countries have a special responsibility for achieving those goals. To get there, we need to stabilize population; more equitably share resources, income, and work; invest in the natural and social capital commons; reform the financial system to better reflect real assets and liabilities; create better measures of progress; reform tax systems to tax "bads" rather than goods; promote technological innovations that support well-being rather than growth; establish "strong democracy," and create a culture of well-being rather than consumption. In other words, a complete makeover.

These policies are mutually supportive and the resulting system is feasible. It is not merely a utopian fantasy. In fact, it is business as usual that is the utopian fantasy. We will have to create something different and better or risk collapse into something far worse.

The substantial challenge is making the transition to a better world in a peaceful and positive way. There is no way to predict the exact path this transition might take, but we hope that painting this picture of a possible end-point and some milestones along the way will help make this choice and this journey a more viable option.

7. References

1. Rockström J, Steffen W, Noone K, Persson Å, Chapin FS, et al. (2009) A safe operating space for humanity. Nature 461: 472-475.

2. Steffen W, Rockström J, Costanza R (2011) How defining planetary boundaries can transform our approach to growth. Solutions 2: 59-65.

3. Crutzen PJ (2002) The effects of industrial and agricultural practices on atmospheric chemistry and climate during the Anthropocene. Journal of Environmental Science and Health, Part A 37: 423-424.

4. Daly HE (2005) Economics in a full world. Scientific American 293: 100-107.

5. UNEP (2011) Towards a green economy: Pathways to sustainable development and poverty eradication—A synthesis for policy makers. France: United Nations Environment Programme.

6. Daly HE (1968) On economics as a life science. Journal of Political Economy 76: 392-406.

7. Costanza R (1991) Ecological economics: The science and management of sustainability: Columbia University Press.

8. Costanza R, dArge R, de Groot R, Farber S, Grasso M, et al. (1997) The value of the world's ecosystem services and natural capital. Nature 387: 253-260.

9. Daly HE, Farley J (2004) Ecological economics: Principles and applications. Island Press.

10. Raskin P, Banuri T, Gallopin G, Gutman P, Hammond A, et al. (2002) Great transition: The promise of lure of the times ahead. Boston: Stockholm Environment Institute.

11. Kasser T (2002) The high price of materialism: The MIT Press.

12. Costanza R, Graumlich L, Steffen W, Crumley C, Dearing J, et al. (2007) Sustainability or collapse: What can we learn from integrating the history of humans and the rest of nature? Ambio 36: 522-527.

13. MEA MEA (2005) Ecosystems and Human Well-Being: Synthesis. Island Press.

14. Easterlin RA (2003) Explaining happiness. Proceedings of the National Academy of Sciences 100: 11176-11183.

15. Layard R (2005) Happiness: Lessons from a new science. New York: The Penguin Press.

16. Frank RH (1999) Luxury fever: Why money fails to satisfy in an era of excess: Simon and Schuster.

17. MEA MEA (2005) Ecosystems and Human Well-Being: Synthesis: Island Press.

18. Sukhdev P, Kumar P (2010) The Economics of Ecosystems and Biodiversity (TEEB). European Communities Brussels.

19. Costanza R, Fisher B, Ali S, Beer C, Bond L, et al. (2007) Quality of life: An approach integrating opportunities, human needs, and subjective well-being. Ecological Economics 61: 267-276.

20. United Nations Development Programme (1998) Human Development Report. Oxford University Press.

21. Diener E, Suh EM (2003) National differences in subjective weil-being. In: Kahneman D, Diener E, Schwarz N, editors. Well-being: The foundations of hedonic psychology. New York: Russell Sage Foundation.

22. Nussbaum M, Glover J (1995) Women, culture, and development: A study of human capabilities. Oxford: Oxford University Press.

23. Costanza R, Fisher B, Ali S, Beer C, Bond L, et al. (2007) Quality of life: An approach integrating opportunities, human needs, and subjective well-being. Ecological Economics 61: 267-276.

24. Azar OH (2004) What sustains social norms and how they evolve? The case of tipping. Journal of Economic Behavior and Organization 54: 49-64.

25. Costanza R (2000) Social goals and the valuation of ecosystem services. Ecosystems 3: 4-10.

26. Third World Network (2012) Statement of the plurinational state of Bolivia at 12th special session of the governing council/global environment ministers forum of the UNEP. Nairobi, Kenya: Third World Network.

27. Hernández-Murillo R, Martinek CJ (2010) The dismal science tackles happiness data. The Regional Economist. pp. 14-15.

28. Costanza R, Hart M, Posner S, Talberth J (2009) Beyond GDP: The need for new measures of progress. Boston, MA: Frederick S. Pardee Center for the Study of the Longer-Range Future.

29. Stiglitz JE, Sen A, Fitoussi JP (2010) Mismeasuring our lives: Why GDP doesn't add up. New York: The New Press.

30. Talberth J, Cobb C, Slattery N (2007) The Genuine Progress Indicator 2006: A tool for sustainable develoment. Oakland, CA: Redefining Progress.

31. Frank RH (2007) Falling behind: How rising inequality harms the middle class: University of California Press.

32. Wilkinson RG, Pickett K (2009) The spirit level: Why greater equality makes societies stronger. New York: Bloomsbury Press.

33. Alperovitz G (2011) America beyond capitalism: Reclaiming our wealth, our liberty, and our democracy. New York: Democracy Collaborative Press.

34. Prugh T, Costanza R, Daly HE (2000) The local politics of global sustainability. Washington, DC: Island Press.

35. Williamson T, Dubb S, Alperovitz G (2010) Climate Change, Community Stability and the Next 150 Million Americans. College Park: The Democracy Collaborative at the University of Maryland.

36. Raworth K (2012) A Safe and Just Space for Humanity: Can we live within the doughnut? : Oxfam International.

37. Costanza R (2000) Visions of alternative (unpredictable) futures and their use in policy analysis. Conservation Ecology 4: 5.

38. Meadows D (2010) Leverage points: Places to intervene in a system. Solutions 1: 41-49.

39. Barber BR (1984) Strong democracy: Participatory politics for a new age. London, U.K.: University of California Press.

40. Barber BR (1998) A place for us: How to make society civil and democracy strong. New York: Hill and Wang.

41. Costanza R, Andrade F, Antunes P, van den Belt M, Boersma D, et al. (1998) Principles for sustainable governance of the oceans. Science 281: 198-199.

42. Beddoe R, Costanza R, Farley J, Garza E, Kent J, et al. (2009) Overcoming systemic roadblocks to sustainability: The evolutionary redesign of worldviews, institutions, and technologies. Proceedings of the National Academy of Sciences 106: 2483-2489.

43. Stern N (2007) The economics of climate change: The Stern review. Cambridge, UK: Cambridge Press.

44. Hansen J, Sato M, Kharecha P, Beerling D, Berner R, et al. (2008) Target atmospheric CO_2: Where should humanity aim? The Open Atmospheric Science Journal 2: 217-231.

45. Food and Agriculture Organization of the United Nations (2009) How to Feed the World in 2050. Rome: UN FAO.

46. Worm B, Barbier EB, Beaumont N, Duffy JE, Folke C, et al. (2006) Impacts of Biodiversity Loss on Ocean Ecosystem Services. Science 314: 787-790.

47. Goodland R, Anhang J (2009) Livestock and climate change: What if the key actors in climate change are cows, pigs and chickens? World Watch 22: 10-19.

48. Simon HA (1981) Man and his tools: Technology and the human condition: Intermediair bibliotheek.

49. Kowalski SP (2002) Golden rice: a case study in intellectual property management and International capacity building. Pierce Law Faculty Scholarship Series Paper 7.

50. De Schutter O (2010) Report submitted by the Special Rapporteur on the right to food. NY: United Nations Human Right Council.

51. Vanloqueren G, Baret PV (2009) How agricultural research systems shape a technological regime that develops genetic engineering but locks out agroecological innovations. Research Policy 38: 971-983.

52. Avato P, Coony J (2008) Accelerating clean energy technology research, development, and deployment. Washington, DC: World Bank.

53. Coy P (2012) The Other U.S. Energy Crisis: Lack of R&D: R&D neglect is holding back innovative energy technologies. Bloomberg Businessweek. New York: Bloomberg L.P.

54. Alston JM, Marra MC, Pardey PG, Wyatt TJ (2000) Research returns redux: a meta-analysis of the returns to agricultural R&D. Australian Journal of Agricultural and Resource Economics 44: 185-215.

55. Brown LR (2011) The New Geopolitics of Food. Foreign Policy. Washington, DC: The FP Group.

56. Bloom DE, Canning D (2004) Global demographic change: Dimensions and economic significance. Population and Development Review 34: 17-51.

57. Birdsall N, Kelley AC, Sinding SW (2003) Population matters: Demographic change, economic growth, and poverty in the developing world. Oxford, UK: Oxford University Press.

58. Cincotta RP, Engelman R, Anastasion D (2003) The security demographic: Population and civil conflict after the Cold War. DTIC Document.

59. Singh S, Darroch J, Ashford L, Vlassoff M (2010) Adding it up: The costs and benefits of investing in family planning and maternal and newborn health. New York: Guttmacher Institute.

60. Department of Economic and Social Affairs UN (2009) What would it take to accelerate fertility decline in the least developed countries?

61. Bongaarts J, Sinding S (2011) Population Policy in Transition in the Developing World. Science 333: 574-576.

62. Bongaarts J (2009) Human population growth and the demographic transition. Philosophical Transactions of the Royal Society B: Biological Sciences 364: 2985-2990.

63. Singh S, Darroch JE, Vlassoff M, Nadeau J (2003) Adding it up: The benefits of investing in sexual and reproductive health care. New York: Guttmacher Institute and United Nations Population Fund (UNFPA).

64. Carr D, Khan M (2004) The unfinished agenda: Meeting the need for family planning in less developed countries. Washington, DC: Population Reference Bureau.

65. Sedgh G, Hussain R, Bankole A, Singh S (2007) Women with an unmet need for contraception in developing countries and their reasons for not using a method. New York: Guttmacher Institute. pp. 5-40.

66. Speidel JJ, Weiss DC, Ethelston SA, Gilbert SM (2009) Population policies, programmes and the environment. Philosophical Transactions of the Royal Society B: Biological Sciences 364: 3049-3065.

67. Ehrlich PR, Ehrlich AH (1991) The population explosion. New York: Simon & Schuster.

68. Wilson EO (2003) The future of life: Vintage.

69. United Nations Development Programme UNEP, World Bank, and World Resources Institute (2003) World resources 2002–2004: Decisions for the Earth: Balance, voice, and power. Washington, DC.

70. Brown LR (2004) Outgrowing the Earth: The food security challenge in an age of falling water tables and rising temperatures. London: Earth Policy Institute.

71. Brown LR, Institute EP (2008) Plan B 3.0: Mobilizing to save civilization. New York: WW Norton.

72. Jackson T (2009) Prosperity without growth: Economics for a finite planet: Earthscan/ James & James.

73. Schor JB (2005) Sustainable consumption and worktime reduction. Journal of Industrial Ecology 9: 37-50.

74. Bell LA, Freeman RB (2001) The incentive for working hard: Explaining hours worked: Differences in the US and Germany. Labour Economics 8: 181-202.

75. Bowles S, Park Y (2005) Emulation, inequality, and work hours: Was Thorsten Veblen right? The Economic Journal 115: F397–F412.

76. Cross G (1993) Of time and money: The making of consumer culture. London: Routledge.

77. Durning A (1992) How much is enough? The consumer society and the future of the Earth. New York: W. W. Norton.

78. Farley J (2010) Ecological Economics. In: Lerch RHaD, editor. The Post Carbon Reader - Managing the 21st Century's Sustainability Crises.

79. Acemoglu D, Robinson J (2009) Foundations of societal inequality. Science 326: 678-679.

80. Daly HE (2010) From a failed-growth economy to a steady-state economy. Solutions 1: 37-43.

81. Almås I, Cappelen AW, Sørensen EØ, Tungodden B (2010) Fairness and the development of inequality acceptance. Science 328: 1176-1178.

82. Fehr E, Falk A (2002) Psychological foundations of incentives. European Economic Review 46: 687-724.

83. Farley J, Costanza R (2002) Envisioning shared goals for humanity: A detailed, shared vision of a sustainable and desirable USA in 2100. Ecological Economics 43: 245-259.

84. Kubiszewski I, Farley J, Costanza R (2010) The production and allocation of information as a good that is enhanced with increased use. Ecological Economics 69: 1344-1354.

85. Hardin G (1968) The Tragedy of the Commons. pp. 1243-1248.

86. Ostrom E (1990) Governing the commons: The evolution of institutions for collective action: Cambridge University Press.

87. Pell D (1989) Common property resources: Ecology and community-based sustainable development; Berkes F, editor. London: Belhaven.

88. Feeny D, Berkes F, McCay BJ, Acheson JM (1990) The tragedy of the commons: Twenty-two years later. Human Ecology 18: 1-19.

89. Barnes P (2006) Capitalism 3.0: A guide to reclaiming the commons. San Francisco, CA: Berrett-Koehler Publishers.

90. Barnes P, Costanza R, Hawken P, Orr D, Ostrom E, et al. (2008) Creating an Earth atmospheric trust. Science 319: 724.

91. Street J (2001) Electronic democracy. International Encyclopedia of the Social & Behavioral Sciences 7: 43-97.

92. Gore A (2007) The assault on reason: Penguin Pr.

93. Smith A (2009) The Internet's role in campaign 2008. Pew Internet & American Life Project 15.

94. López R, Galinato GI (2007) Should governments stop subsidies to private goods? Evidence from rural Latin America. Journal of Public Economics 91: 1071-1094.

95. Daly HE (2008) Ecological economics and sustainable development, selected essays of Herman Daly. Cornwall: Edward Elgar Publishing.

96. Daly HE, Cobb JB, Jr. (1994) For the common good: Redirecting the economy toward community, the environment, and a sustainable future; 2nd edition. Boston: Beacon Press.

97. Gaffney M (2009) The hidden taxable capacity of land: enough and to spare. International Journal of Social Economics 36: 328-411.

98. Goldstein M (2011) Paulson, at $4.9 billion, tops hedge fund earner list. Reuters: Thomson Reuters.

99. Kubiszewski I, Costanza R (2012) A Fair Share of the Information Commons. In: Murray J, Cawthorne G, Dey C, Andrew C, editors. Enough for all forever: A handbook for learning about sustainability. Champaign, Illinois: Common Ground Publishing.

100. Calomiris CW (2010) Financial innovation, regulation, and reform. In: Spence M, Leipziger D, editors. Globalization and growth: Implications for a post-crisis world. Washington DC: The World Bank.

101. Anderson V (1991) Alternative economic indicators. London: Routledge.

102. MaxNeef M (1995) Economic growth and quality of life: A threshold hypothesis. Ecological Economics 15: 115-118.

103. Boulding K (1968) Beyond economics: essays on society, religion, and ethics. Ann Arbor, MI: University of Michigan Press.

104. Farley J, Aquino A, Daniels A, Moulaert A, Lee D, et al. (2010) Global mechanisms for sustaining and enhancing PES schemes. Ecological Economics 69: 2075-2084.

105. New Economics Foundation (2008) Triple crunch: Joined-up solutions to financial chaos, oil decline and climate change to transform the economy London: New Economics Foundation.

106. New Economics Foundation (2009) The cuts won't work: The second report of the Green New Deal Group. London: New Economics Foundation.

107. Alperovitz G, Faux J (1984) Rebuilding America: A blueprint for the new economy. Oxford: PsychoBabel Books.

108. Arrow K, Dasgupta P, Goulder L, Daily G, Ehrlich P, et al. (2004) Are we consuming too much? The Journal of Economic Perspectives 18: 147-172.

109. Schor JB (2005) Prices and quantities: Unsustainable consumption and the global economy. Ecological Economics 55: 309-320.

110. Kallis G (2011) In defence of degrowth. Ecological Economics 70: 873-880.

111. Frank R (2007) Falling Behind: How Rising Inequality Harms the Middle Class. Berkeley: University of California Press.

112. van den Bergh JCJM (2011) Environment versus growth — A criticism of "degrowth" and a plea for "a-growth". Ecological Economics 70: 881-890.

113. Sorrell S (2007) The Rebound Effect: an assessment of the evidence for economy-wide energy savings from improved energy efficiency. Sussex Energy Group for the Technology and Policy Assessment function of The New Economics Foundation UK Energy Research Centre.

114. Polimeni JM, Mayumi K, Giampietro M, Blake Alcott (2008) The Jevons Paradoxnext and the myth of resource efficiency improvements. Sterling, VA: Earthscan.

115. Kallis G (2011) In defence of degrowth. Ecological Economics.

116. Knight R, Schor JB, Rose E (In Progress) Work hours, consumption, and climate change: A cross-national analysis of OECD countries, 1970-2007.

117. Victor P (2010) Questioning economic growth. Nature 468: 370-371.

118. Jackson T, Victor P (2011) Productivity and work in the 'green economy': Some theoretical reflections and empirical tests. Environmental Innovation and Societal Transitions 1: 101-108.

119. Schor J (2011) Combating consumerism and capitalism: A decade of no logo. WSQ: Women's Studies Quarterly 38: 299-301.

120. Howarth RB (1996) Status effects and environmental externalities. Ecological Economics 16: 25-34.

121. Victor PA, Rosenbluth G (2007) Managing without growth. Ecological Economics 61: 492-504.

122. Frank R (2012) Higher taxes help the richest, too. New York Times. New York.

123. Nørgård JS. Sustainable degrowth through more amateur economy; 2010; Barcelona.

124. Martínez-Alier J, Pascual U, Vivien FD, Zaccai E (2010) Sustainable de-growth: Mapping the context, criticisms and future prospects of an emergent paradigm. Ecological Economics 69: 1741-1747.

125. Jackson T (2007) Sustainable consumption. In: Atkinson G, Dietz S, Neumayer E, editors. Handbook of sustainable development. Cornwall: Edward Elgar Publishing. pp. 254.

126. Gannon Z, Lawson N (2009) The advertising effect: How do we get the balance of advertising right. London: Compass.

127. Costanza R, Farley J, Kubiszewski I (2010) Adapting institutions for life in a full world. In: Assadourian E, editor. 2010 State of the World. Washington, DC: The Worldwatch Institute.

128. Swann RS (1972) The community land trust: A guide to a new model for land tenure in America. Cambridge, MA: Center for Community Economic Development.

129. Davis JE, Jacobus R (2008) The city-CLT partnership: Municipal support for community land trusts. Cambridge, MA: Lincoln Institute of Land Policy.

130. Adams JS, Victurine R (2011) Permanent Conservation Trusts: A Study of the Long-Term Benefits of Conservation Endowments. Conservation Trust Funds.

131. Seeland K, Dübendorfer S, Hansmann R (2009) Making friends in Zurich's urban forests and parks: The role of public green space for social inclusion of youths from different cultures. Forest Policy and Economics 11: 10-17.

132. van den Berg AE, Maas J, Verheij RA, Groenewegen PP (2010) Green space as a buffer between stressful life events and health. Social Science & Medicine 70: 1203-1210.

133. Mitchell R, Popham F (2008) Effect of exposure to natural environment on health inequalities: an observational population study. The Lancet 372: 1655-1660.

134. RGGI Inc. (2011) Investment of Proceeds from RGGI CO_2 Allowances. Regional Greenhouse Gas Initiative. Online: http://www.rggi.org/docs/Investment_of_RGGI_Allowance_Proceeds.pdf.

135. Cowart R (2008) Carbon caps and efficiency resources: How climate legislation can mobilize efficiency and lower the cost of greenhouse gas emission reduction. Vermont Law Review 33: 201-223.

136. Capoor K, Ambrosi P (2009) State and Trends of the Carbon Market 2009. Washington DC: World Bank.

137. Burtraw D, Mansur E (1999) The environmental effects of SO_2 trading and banking. Environmental Science and Technology 33: 3489–3494.

138. Bradshaw MJ (1988) Regions and regionalism in the United States. Jackson, MS: University Press of Mississippi.

139. Collits P (2007) Planning for regions in Australia. In: Thompson S, editor. Planning Australia: An Overview of Urban and Regional Planning. Melbourne: Cambridge University Press.

140. Glasson J, Marshall T (2007) Regional planning. Milton Park: Routledge.

141. Hodge G, Robinson IM (2002) Planning Canadian regions. Vancouver: University of British Columbia Press.

142. Costanza R, Farley J (2010) What should be done with the revenues from a carbon cap and auction systems? Solutions 1: 33.

143. UNEP (2009) Global green new deal: A policy brief. United Natins Environment Programme.

144. Smith B, Costello T, Brecher J (2009) Bailing out the planet. Transnational Institute.

145. Kirk DJ (2010) Allocating Vermont's Trust: Dividends or public investment from carbon cap and auction revenues. Burlington: University of Vermont.

146. Barnes P, McKibben W (2010) A simple market mechanism to clean up our economy. Solutions 1: 30-40.

147. Kunkel CM, Kammen DM (2011) Design and implementation of carbon cap and dividend policies. Energy Policy 39: 477-486.

148. Coy P (2010) The Other U.S. Energy Crisis: Lack of R&D: R&D neglect is holding back innovative energy technologies. Bloomberg Business Week

149. Nauclér T, Enkvist PA (2009) Pathways to a low-carbon economy: Version 2 of the global greenhouse gas abatement cost curve. McKinsey & Company. pp. 26-31.

150. Golden L, Wiens-Tuers B (2006) To your happiness? Extra hours of labor supply and worker well-being. Journal of Socio-Economics 35: 382-397.

151. Kasser T, Brown KW (2003) On time, happiness, and ecological footprints. In: DeGraaf J, editor. Take back your time!: Fighting overwork and time poverty in America San Francisco: Berrett-Koehler Publishers. pp. 107-112.

152. Kasser T, Sheldon K (2009) Time Affluence as a Path toward Personal Happiness and Ethical Business Practice: Empirical Evidence from Four Studies. Journal of Business Ethics 84: 243-255.

153. Binswanger M (2001) Technological progress and sustainable development: what about the rebound effect? Ecological Economics 36: 119-132.

154. Jalas M (2002) A time use perspective on the materials intensity of consumption. Ecological Economics 41: 109-123.

155. Nässén J, Larsson J, Holmberg J (2009) The effect of work hours on energy use: A micro-analysis of time and income effects. Proceedings to ACEEE Summer Study, La Colle sur Loup, France: 1-6.

156. Rosnick D, Weisbrot M (2007) Are Shorter Work Hours Good for the Environment? A Comparison of US and European Energy Consumption. International Journal of Health Services 37: 405-417.

157. Otterbach S (2010) Mismatches Between Actual and Preferred Work Time: Empirical Evidence of Hours Constraints in 21 Countries. Journal of Consumer Policy 33: 143-161.

158. Sanne C (1992) How much work? Futures 24: 23-36.

159. Schor J (2010) The Work-Sharing Boom: Exit Ramp to a New Economy? . Yes! Magazine. Bainbridge Island, Washington: Positive Futures Network.

160. Redman CL (1999) Human impact on ancient environments. Tucson: University of Arizona Press.

161. Schellnhuber HJ, Crutzen PJ, Clark WC, Claussen M, Held H (2004) Earth system analysis for sustainability. Berlin, Germany: The MIT Press and Freie Universitat Berlin.

162. Steffen W, Sanderson A, Tyson PD, Jager J, Matson PM, et al. (2004) Global change and the Earth system: a planet under pressure. Heidelberg, Germany: Springer.

163. Diamond J (2005) Guns, Germs, and Steel: The Fates of Human Societies: W. W. Norton.

164. Hibbard KA, Costanza R, Crumley C, van der Leeuw S, Aulenbach S, et al. (2010) Developing an Integrated History and Future of People on Earth (IHOPE): Research Plan. Stockholm, Sweden: IGBP Secretariat. 40 pp.

165. Weiss H, Bradley RS (2001) What drives societal collapse? Science 291: 609-610.

166. O'Neill DW (In Press) Measuring progress in the degrowth transition to a steady state economy. Ecological Economics.

167. Costanza R, Leemans R, Boumans R, Gaddis E (2007) Integrated global models. In: Costanza R, Graumlich L, Steffen W, editors. Sustainability or collapse? An integrated history and future of people on earth. Cambridge, MA: MIT Press. pp. 417-446.

168. Meadows DH, Meadows DL, Randers J, Behrens WW (1972) The limits to growth: Signet.

169. Meadows DH, Meadows DL, Randers J (1992) Beyond the limits: confronting global collapse, envisioning a sustainable future: Chelsea Green Pub.

170. Meadows DH, Randers J, Meadows DL (2004) Limits to growth: the 30-year update. White River Junction, VT: Chelsea Green Publishing Company. 368 pp.

171. Economist (1997) Plenty of gloom. Economist. pp. 19-20.

172. Turner GM (2008) A comparison of The Limits to Growth with 30 years of reality. Global Environmental Change-Human and Policy Dimensions 18: 397-411.

173. Cole HSD, Freeman C, Jahoda M, Pavitt KLR (1973) Models of Doom: A Critique of the Limits to Growth. New York: Universe Pub.

174. Costanza R, Daly M, Folke C, Hawken P, Holling CS, et al. (2000) Managing our environmental portfolio. Bioscience 50: 149-155.

175. Boumans R, Costanza R, Farley J, Wilson MA, Portela R, et al. (2002) Modeling the dynamics of the integrated earth system and the value of global ecosystem services using the GUMBO model. Ecological Economics 41: 529-560.

176. Victor PA (2008) Managing without growth: slower by design, not disaster. Cheltenham, UK: Edward Elgar Publishing.

www.ingramcontent.com/pod-product-compliance
Lightning Source LLC
Chambersburg PA
CBHW050100220326
41599CB00049B/7218